Always Getting Ready *Upterrlainarluta*

Lola Evan, Peter Evan, Wassillie Evan, and David E. David, from Kwethluk.

John Abraham and George Chimugak, Toksook Bay seal hunters, study ice conditions.

Always Getting Ready   *Upterrlainarluta*

Yup'ik Eskimo Subsistence in Southwest Alaska

Photographs by **James H. Barker**

Text by James H. Barker with the assistance of Robin Barker

Foreword by Mary C. Pete

University of Washington Press   Seattle & London

Al and Helen Wasuli, Kotlik.

Contents

Richard Long, Betty Guy, Molly Owens, and host David Nicolai, Kwethluk.

Foreword

On Our Own Terms

IN 1984, I WENT TO STEBBINS, THE COMMUNITY where I grew up, to attend the annual potlatch with Kotlik, a neighboring community. As usual, the community hall was packed with people every night of the potlatch. The space of the dance floor constantly renegotiated its compromise with the audience, especially the excited children sitting in front of a concentric circle of people several bodies deep. Intermittent announcements by elders included requests to parents to use more discipline with their kids, a plea that brought temporary results.

It just so happened that Jim Barker also attended the same event to take pictures for the Alaska State Council on the Arts. Many other cameras flashed throughout the event, including my own. Every so often, I would hear a genuinely curious comment from someone within earshot—"The big *kass'aq* photographer seems to be everywhere, one minute he's here, next to me, camera clicking, and the next minute he's across the room. How does he get around all the bodies so quickly?" Interestingly, my own and my relatives' slides of the potlatch confirm Jim's seeming omnipresence. In many a frame, there he is in the background: in a crouch scooting along the edge of the dance floor; carefully picking his way to another vantage point, balancing on one long leg as he is stepping over oblivious and otherwise engaged spectators; laughing, open-mouthed, with the rest of us; or a study in concentration, brows furrowed as he scrutinizes the scene for a shot. But always, one or all of the cameras hanging around his neck is in hand, either held up against his chest and out of the way, while he moves above or through the crowd, or part way up to, or completely in front of, his face.

During the day, Jim visited and talked to people. He appeared in my parents' home one day and ate a bowl of *akutaq* and drank a cup of tea. He commented that these were among many bowls of food and cups of tea that he had accepted: it would seem inappropriate to refuse. He said that it was easier to deal privately with all the ingested food by walking more and eating less when out of the village, than by rudely providing excuses for not appreciating the proffered food. As he left, a visiting aunt said, "*Atawauluni augna kass'aq. Avatemtini piuraraqami, wangkuta piciyaraput aturaqluki, qessakinguarpeknani.*" Meaning, "He is beneficial [fortunate, a blessing], that white man. When he is among us he uses our ways, not pretending to be disinclined to act [in our ways, on our own terms]."

Before the potlatch, I had already formed an unqualified respect for Jim's work; I'd spent enough time captivated by his photographs and, when I could eventually afford it, bought some of his work for my house or for gifts to friends and family. The potlatch experience and those comments about Jim substantiated for me the congruity of the man behind the work. When he worked among us, he did seem to immerse himself, to be everywhere without "getting in the way." He seemed ready to learn about anything when someone was ready to offer the information or the insight, much as a good ethnographer is supposed to be. His unobtrusive style showed in the photographs. In his work, he has captured Yup'iks unabashedly being Yup'iks. Many times, we catch ourselves staring at Jim's photographs around the delta, where they serve as backdrops to the news studio at KYUK, the local public radio/television station, or the Kuskokwim College campus reception area and lounge. Invariably, the observer has a faint smile of appreciation, recognition, or interest. Photographs hanging in village schools taken by local amateurs will hint of an attempt at imitating Jim's style. As my aunt said, he both captures us and shows us "on our own terms."

Coming to Terms

Central Yup'ik Eskimos are named for the language and the term with which they call themselves—*yup'iit*, meaning "real people." They number about 20,000 of an estimated total of 25,000 people in some seventy communities scattered along the coast from Bristol Bay to Norton Sound and several hundred miles up the major rivers. The focus of Jim Barker's work and my expertise is among the Yup'iks of the Yukon-Kuskokwim Delta, excluding the Bristol Bay region, which has had a different historical experience. Communities in the Yukon-Kuskokwim Delta range in size from 60 to 4,500 people, with Bethel, the transportation and service center, as the largest and quite cosmopolitan community. There are no roads between communities, but travel in the region is extensive by boat in months of open water and by snowmachine or dog sled in the winter. The frozen Kuskokwim River provides the closest thing to a highway linking villages surrounding Bethel.

The first and frequently the only effective language of elders and some children in many communities is Yup'ik; Yup'ik-speaking children encounter English on television and in school, and middle-aged and young adults are commonly bilingual. Opportunities for wage employment are scarce, often intermittent and seasonal in nature, resulting in the lowest average incomes in the nation coupled with a very high cost of living. Subsistence output in the region is among the most productive in the state—annual per capita harvest rates of 1,100 pounds of wild fish and game have been documented for some communities in the region. Subsistence production is the most consistently stable and reliable sector of the local economy. Many of the photographs here attest to the critical importance of subsistence. Subsistence activities are carried out by, shared among, and reinforce the strength and significance of Yup'ik families.

Yup'iks were the last of Alaska's Native groups to have sustained contact with non-Natives; one simple reason was that the shallow Bering Sea along the Yukon-Kuskokwim Delta inhibited effective exploration by deep draft vessels.

Yup'iks have experienced many changes since historic contact, changes ranging from subtle to drastic, seemingly neutral to decidedly biased, and initially unintentional to calculated. This is not to say that Yup'iks on their own would not experience change, as it is a normal state for all peoples and cultures, but the past century did produce special conditions and set unusual processes in motion.

Many of the highlights of the past century have been analyzed from many perspectives. Technological and material introductions, easily discussed and generally appreciated, are the most tangible evidence of change. Adjustments imposed by new laws and regulations have generated the most speculation and scrutiny. However, these are usually not the issues Yup'iks examine among themselves for decisive and far-reaching effects. Yup'iks talk more about the effects of disease epidemics, the reorganization of residential patterns and relations between the men and women, prohibition of many important sociopolitical and religious ceremonies, management schemes imposed on natural resources, and differential attitudes through time toward the Native language by missionaries and educational systems. I will address a few of these issues here.

In the mid-1800s, Yup'iks were organized into approximately twenty kin-based societal groups or *tungelquqellriit*, meaning "those who share ancestors (are related)." The most socially significant and economically effective units of membership were related, extended (three generations) families or *ilakellriit*. Each named society was specified by a set of non-gendered human names which circulated between the living and the dead, thus continuing a thread of life for the human dead, and through the generations. Each society defined its preferred marriage universe, generally spoke a distinctive dialect, practiced a particular annual seasonal round of subsistence activities in recognized access to and use of a specific area, celebrated social, political, and religious ceremonies together, often cooperating to host or to be guests to neighboring societies in social and political events. In the time of wars, societies cooperated with other societies and in fact sought allies from other, usually neighboring, societies.

Societies were known to relate to their neighbors in different ways. For example, the people of Russian Mission—situated in a popular travel route between the Kuskokwim and Yukon drainages and next to Athabaskan Indians—claimed humility as their prevalent attitude toward their neighbors. Ancestors of Hooper Bay and Chevak people were noted for their aggressiveness.

This societal organization has been affected by changes in demography, settlement pattern, resource abundance and distribution, and gender roles and relations. Devastating epidemics since 1900 left a frightened people with many orphans, unsettled about their relationships with each other, their surrounding resources, and their spiritual world. Local traditional means to address and appease forces such as illness and resource availability were forever shaken. Governmental attempts to alleviate the effects of epidemics, particularly the tuberculosis outbreak in the early to mid-1900s, are viewed with mixed feelings, although saving lives of kin was always appreciated. Infected people were often taken to out-of-state sanitariums, away from their families, to return months or years later and find themselves and their homes inevitably different. This aggressive and disruptive treatment, along with improved provision of health services, has meant that many areas of the Yukon-Kuskokwim Delta are returning to what are thought to be the local population levels of pre-contact time.

Even prior to contact, some Yup'ik societies became non-functional. Such a society's members would essentially have been subsumed by another society and its use area overtaken as well. Dwindling membership, subsistence hardship usually blamed on members' disrespect of resources or lax attention to prescribed and proscribed rituals, and failure to uphold obligations to neighboring societies signaled the demise of a society.

Many current Yup'ik communities or closely situated communities concede to societal boundaries in their composition, prevailing marriage patterns, land use, and linguistic dialect. Each has had its own history and relationships with other societies and its own response to outside change agents.

Thus each community has developed a distinctive character and reputation. Some communities have reactivated aspects of their relationship through dance festivals, as photographs in this book so aptly portray.

Traditionally, men and women had separate residences—men and boys from the age of about six years lived, worked, and socialized through the institution of the qasgiq, men's house (now used to refer to the steambath house), which was also the settlement's ceremonial and political center. Women, their daughters and daughters-in-law, and children lived in extended-family dwellings. This separation of the sexes implied and actuated complex cultural, social, and political rules and relations between the sexes, dissected by differential prestige afforded individuals by age and the sex, role, and personality of deceased namesakes. Men and women certainly were not equal by modern feminist standards, but their relations and respective roles differed from those practiced today. In many aspects, they were viewed as complementary (men hunted and women processed), though, for reasons of survival, each individual was expected to be self-sufficient. Young adults (often pre-teen girls) were arranged in marriage. The marriage tie was fragile, especially when childless; thus, many people had serial marriages without negative stigma. By mutual consent, individuals maintained kinship relations with families of their previous spouses, particularly if there were children. This resulted in societies with complex kinship networks and sources of assistance. Many elders, both men and women, remember the prior way (the qasgiq) with fond nostalgia not only for its separation of the sexes but for its child-rearing patterns.

The importance of children in Yup'ik society and culture, especially from the perspective of elderly women, deserves mention. These women note that until about mid-century, women gave birth to many babies, but relatively few survived infancy. Mothers often went into deep depression from these deaths and sometimes were reluctant to invest emotionally in their babies. Women speak with veneration of the traditional system, which provided love and care for infants and children whose mourning mothers were incapacitated by grief; someone always kept the baby "next to her skin," and male children were under close supervision of the men. The ceremony celebrating a child's first catch and contribution to the family larder was often considered to signal probable survival to adulthood.

The sexually separated residence pattern and the child-rearing system it maintained was one of the first traditions that missionaries and educational institutions sought to abolish and replace with nuclear family–based residential units. Yup'iks appreciate the mitigation of high infant mortality; large families with many children are viewed as blessed and truly wealthy. But the traditional support system for families has changed and difficulties of the times are often reflected in destructive social problems.

In another arena of interactive change, since the 1960s non-Native governmental agencies have increased their intervention in harvests and use of natural resources in the delta. This process has essentially paralleled the development of commercial salmon fisheries. In the resultant, continuing public debate over subsistence practices, many Yup'ik have been active in providing input to agency processes and plans of management, and these negotiations reveal differing philosophies about relationships among people and between humans and natural resources, between the Yup'ik world view and western science and wildlife management. The chasm is wide and deep, and Yup'iks view what is at stake as their most important challenge. The basic western scientific tenet that wildlife can be managed draws incredulity from some Yup'iks; humans should not be so presumptuous and arrogant lest animals and fish make themselves scarce. In the hunting and processing of wild fish and game, Yup'iks actuate their relationship with the natural world. Some expressions of these relationships seem esoteric today, fractured and out of context, especially to youth. Still, there are Yup'ik men who silently and gratefully provide a drink of fresh water to a seal, believing that the seal offered itself to the hunter because he would assure proper and respectful dispatch and processing, beginning with the quenching of its

thirst. For many Yup'iks, subsistence activities teach children much more than hunting and fishing; they convey respect and proper conduct toward the land and water and animals and other humans; they promote satisfaction from hard work and contribution to the kin group. For many Yup'iks, subsistence goes beyond mere economy—it is a vital way of life and a source of pride and identity.

Yup'iks are keen participants in the public discussions about natural resource management. The world is getting smaller and more and more diverse groups have vested interests in the resources on which Yup'iks rely. Yup'iks present their wishes and views, sometimes with trepidation when a closely and deeply held belief is sure to bring skepticism. I have seen elders sweat at the prospect of publicly suggesting to fisheries managers that the discarding of by-caught (prohibited) species may be the cause of fish shortages; fish stocks are withholding themselves from Yup'ik nets because not all human beings along the vast harvest network are exercising proper respect for these fish. Even with the frustration of linguistic and philosophical misunderstandings in these exchanges, Yup'iks seize the opportunities to exercise some self-determination.

In many ways, Yup'iks seem to be coming to terms with these vast changes. The business of taking stock, seeing where we have been and where we might go from here, keeps us busy. Always, Yup'iks treasure the ability to find and express the humor in life. I think this comes out in the photographs as well as Jim Barker's observations of us. It is a fascinating and provocative time to be a Yup'ik in the Yukon-Kuskokwim Delta. Fortunately, many facets of this stimulating time enjoy expression in this book of photographs and the Barkers' interactions with Yup'iks in the Yukon-Kuskokwim Delta.

Mary C. Pete

Bethel, Alaska
July 1992

Preface

WHEN I FIRST CAME TO THE YUKON-Kuskokwim Delta, I felt that I had arrived either at the beginning of the world where no mountains had pushed up yet, or at the end of the world where all the mountains were eroded flat. Newcomers are struck by the clear view of level horizon in every direction and by the full half-sphere sky. Why I was drawn to such utter flatness I can't say. Certainly the region's remoteness, four hundred miles from the nearest connecting road, and its location on the Bering Sea coast intrigued me.

I first visited Bethel, the hub community on the Kuskokwim River, for three weeks during the winter of 1970. During that first visit I was given the loan of a snowmachine and a flight map so that I could visit a nearby village eighteen miles away. I was traveling alone on a noisy old machine, quite terrified that the thing might quit and strand me far from town in the bleak winter whiteness on the Kuskokwim River. I wondered what had ever possessed me. Then I noticed a dog team coming toward me. As we passed, I spotted the driver sitting contentedly in his sled covered by a large skin of some sort. He had a big grin on his face as his team trotted on down the river. I was astonished to realize that Yup'ik people were living quite comfortably in this region that I perceived to be so cold and desolate. I wanted to know who they were.

It wasn't until three years later that I could give the delta further attention. I was invited to do a photographic project for the Yukon-Kuskokwim Heath Corporation, which involved traveling to some of the villages for a few months during the summer. A year later, I moved to the delta with a firm resolve to know more about the people and their land.

At first I worked for KYUK, a bilingual public radio and television station in Bethel. For ten years I was a volunteer reading the news on television, so my face was familiar to almost everyone. Often when I stepped off the plane in a remote village I was welcomed with a big grin, "Hey, you're mister KYUK!" After a couple of years, the native corporation noticed my photographs and hired me to produce numerous booklets addressing the concerns of the villages and the region.

My wife Robin and I met in Bethel. She had grown up on the East Coast, while I was from the west. We both traveled extensively throughout the delta, sometimes together but more often in separate jobs, I photographing and she working with young children. In 1980 I received a small grant from the Alaska State Council on the Arts and another grant in 1982 from the Alaska Humanities Forum, both allowing me to continue my documentation. Sometimes my work for the native corporation took me to the villages but much of the time I simply traveled and worked when time and money allowed. We eventually bought a home in Bethel, and our son Eric was born in the Public Health Service hospital in 1981. We spent thirteen years in Bethel, and I return as often as I can. The photographs here span the years between 1973 and 1992.

Photographing people and representing them truthfully is difficult work. As mechanical and inhibiting as the camera seems, the act of taking photographs sharpens my observations and feelings. I notice the strength of a person's personality when I am framing and waiting for that moment when there is coherency between expression, gesture, and environment. Although I often shoot very quickly to capture those fleeting moments, I've always preferred to take my time getting my camera in hand, working slowly so that I can begin to think like a participant.

When traveling, I always wrote extensive notes. My initial reason for writing was to keep track of names and events and to sharpen my observational skills. Much of the text here is derived from these field notes. Most of the quotes I wrote down as soon as possible after my conversations, paying careful attention to getting the words as exact as memory and my on-the-spot jottings would allow. These quotes are written here in quotation marks. Quotes from taped interviews are noted as such. Statements from documents and recorded testimony are also specifically referenced.

Readers will note that most Yup'ik words are italicized. Yup'ik names of people and places used commonly by English speakers are not, most having been anglicized. Yup'ik words here are spelled using the newly standardized orthography (Jacobson 1984) but they have sometimes been given English plurals to avoid awkwardness.

My conversations with people were usually along practical lines centering on subsistence: how something was done, who did it, how did they used to do it. I wanted to know how living close to the natural environment might shape people in their relationships with each other and with the land. I asked about the ebb and flow of food resources and listened to people's fears about natural events that might disturb the expected return of game. They were confident that if natural forces alone affected the presence of food sources, their needs would be provided for.

This book represents the Yup'iks in different villages around the delta as they busy themselves at a year of subsistence. I have not tried to describe the people and their subsistence activities in full technical detail nor have I tried especially to recapture the past. The book begins in the spring with seal hunting and ends with community celebrations in the winter. I have drawn on the many years of photographs to make this seasonal cycle, so no one actual year is represented. Also, no one village would be involved in all of the activities described here. Habitats and subsistence activities vary greatly from one area to another, and in the space of a few pages here I move from the coast to the inland rivers, from the Kuskokwim to the Yukon.

I set out in the early 1970s to document the experience of life in a subsistence culture. Through my work I wanted to see how living close to the environment would shape people in their relationships with each other and with the land. I have always tried to make sure that my photographs would be used in a way that would support the Yup'ik's concern for the environment and for their culture. I realize that I have responded most to people at their best, looking for moments when the people I visited and traveled with were most at peace with themselves and with each other, when they were most thoughtful, intelligent, and vital. Thus I hope that this book presents those aspects of the life and people of the delta as they search for their own future.

This is not an attempt to give a complete picture of life on the delta, quite an impossible undertaking. This is, more simply, a selection of photos of people who have a unique style of living that I care very much about. These are people who seemed very different from me at first. When there is a moment of real connection or a sense of understanding, then, perhaps because we are different, I have a sense of catching something universal. I make these particular pictures not to show others something new or foreign. I hope instead to strike a chord of familiarity.

James H. Barker
May 1992

Always Getting Ready *Upterrlainarluta*

"All through the year we are getting ready; getting ready for fishing, for berry picking, for potlatches, getting ready for winter. We are always getting ready to go somewhere to get foods. And because we are so religious, you know, we are always getting ready for the next life."—Agnes Kelly Bostrom

I am told that being ever prepared, upterrlainarluta, is a common caution from Yup'ik elders to young people, whether they are preparing for fishing or a trip to the city. Implicit is the understanding that one must be wise in knowing what to prepare for and equally wise in being prepared for the unknowable. Upterrlainarluta is what this book is about.

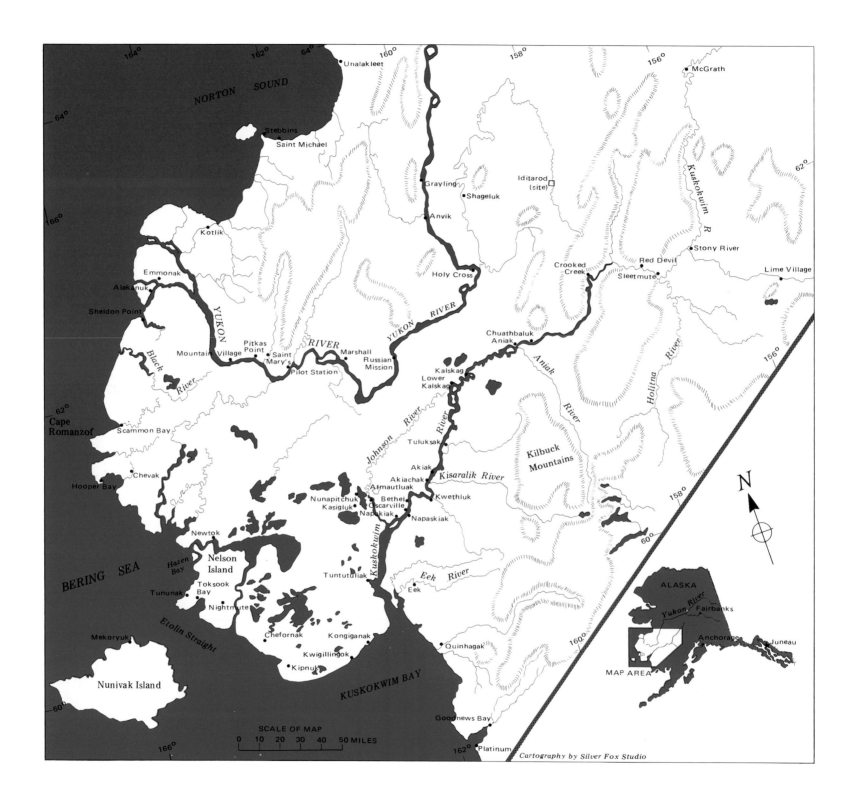

NORTON SOUND

Unalakleet

McGrath

Stebbins
Saint Michael

Grayling

Iditarod
(site)

Shageluk

Kotlik

Anvik

Stony River

Emmonak

Holy Cross

Red Devil

Alakanuk

Crooked
Creek

Sleetmute

Lime Village

Sheldon Point

YUKON

Chuathbaluk
Aniak

Aniak

Cape
Romanzof

Mountain Village

Pitkas
Point

RIVER

Marshall

Black

River

Saint
Mary's

Russian
Mission

YUKON   RIVER

River

Holitna

Pilot Station

Kalskag
Lower
Kalskag

Scammon Bay

Johnson   River

Tuluksak

Kilbuck
Mountains

River

Chevak

Akiak

Kisaralik River

Hooper Bay

Akiachak
Atmautluak

Nunapitchuk
Kasigluk

Bethel
Oscarville

Kwethluk

Newtok

Napakiak

Napaskiak

BERING   SEA

Hazen
Bay

Nelson
Island

Kuskokwim

Toksook
Bay

Tununak

Tuntutuliak

Eek   River

Nightmute

Eek

Mekoryuk

Chefornak

Kongiganak

Quinhagak

Kwigillingok

Nunivak Island

Kipnuk

KUSKOKWIM BAY

Etolin Straight

ALASKA

Yukon River

Fairbanks

Anchorage

Juneau

MAP AREA

SCALE OF MAP
0 10 20 30 40 50 MILES

Goodnews Bay

Platinum

Cartography by Silver Fox Studio

Kuskokwim R

N

14

A Point of Departure

Ayagneq

Kuskokwim River, below Bethel.

ALASKA'S TWO LARGEST RIVERS EMERGE FROM the interior and come within 25 miles of each other before bending apart for the final 200 meandering miles to the Bering Sea. The Kuskokwim and Yukon river waters carry immense quantities of silt eroded from the interior. Over eons this silt has filled in to form an expansive, flat delta. The delta now is a region of subarctic tundra covered with a mixture of moss and grasses that float on a permanently frozen layer of silt or "permafrost." Stunted willows, cottonwoods, and spruce line the rivers in some inland areas, but for the most part the delta is treeless. From the air the region looks like a tenuous compromise that the land has made with the sea. Small melt lakes with no inlet or outlet crowd the spaces left by the web of lakes, rivers, and sloughs. In summer when the land is soft and spongy, the only possible surface travel is by boat.

At a Bureau of Land Management hearing in 1975 Nick O. Nick, from the village of Nunapitchuk, described the delta: "Our land is not the same as the land in the lower 48. I've seen the outside, it's nice and sturdy land. However, here in the Kuskokwim area, here in the lower area, not the upper area, it's different, it's bad. But it's good with its fish, our subsistence. This area is different. The land in this area is not sturdy, it's soft and part of it is like quicksand. It's like that" (Nunam Kitlusisti 1976:2).

The delta is about the size of Kansas. Most maps of the region will show few signs of habitation in this fan-shaped area. However, the delta supports a firmly established population of Eskimo people. They are now the largest group of Alaska Natives to live on their traditional lands, over twenty thousand people in fifty villages. They are Yup'iks, a Bering Sea Eskimo group who speak a different language from that spoken by the northern Inuit.

The climate of the delta is moderated by the Bering Sea. Except in parts of the delta that are closer to the state's interior, the winter temperatures usually do not register below minus 30° F, but these temperatures, combined with constant winds, frequently generate chill factors near 100 below. Summer temperatures are also moderated by the sea

with readings averaging in the 50s and lower 60s. The wind and weather can change quickly. One never leaves home without a coat even in the summer, and safe travel in the winter requires much emergency gear and survival skills.

"Freezeup" marks the beginning of winter when the river ice forms, usually in the middle of October. This can occur very quickly if a cold snap settles in. One year at Bethel only five days separated the use of boats and the safe landing of light planes on the river ice. "Breakup," when the ice moves out, marks the beginning of summer. In the lower Kuskokwim River this occurs about the middle of May, with the Yukon following a week or two later. The dramatic changes at freezeup and breakup help to create the feeling that there are just two seasons in the delta, winter and summer.

The Eskimo have developed a culture adapted to coastal living. The sleek low kayak, spears, darts, and harpoons are efficiently designed for the hunting of sea mammals. But as populations in the delta increased over the precontact period and more land was required to effectively harvest foods, the Yup'iks moved and settled inland up the rivers. There they took advantage of the abundant fish stocks on the Kuskokwim and Yukon rivers and developed relatively comfortable contacts with the Athabaskan Indians in the interior region. These riverine Yup'iks have developed a sub-culture based on the specific living requirements of inland river life. On the Kuskokwim Yup'ik is spoken from the coast up to the village of Sleetmute and on the Yukon Yup'ik is spoken up to Russian Mission.

Throughout the period of early contact with European cultures, from the 1820s through the 1860s, the delta remained relatively isolated. In this region the Bering Sea coast is shallow and not frequented by whales. Whalers passed by in search of more productive waters further north. The abundant fish and the great variety of marine and mammal life sustained a high population that helped the group to survive the devastating epidemics introduced by the Europeans during early contact. As a result the culture of the delta remained more stable than that of the smaller coastal groups to the north. Today, Yup'ik culture and language remain strong in the region and at this point the majority of villages are bilingual.

The first Europeans to frequent Alaska were Russian fur hunters who settled the Aleutian chain and the southeastern coastline in the middle 1700s. In 1799 the Russian American Company was formed by the Tsar and permanent forts and trading posts were established in the Aleutian chain, at Kodiak Island and Sitka. The company also established a trading post and a Russian Orthodox mission in the Nushegak area of Bristol Bay, to the southeast of the delta. The Nushegak agents, hearing of the abundance of beaver along the Kuskokwim, began trading on the river in 1830. In 1841 they built Kolmakovskiy Redoubt 250 miles upriver from the bay, above the present village of Chuathbaluk.

To the northwest, the Russians established two posts in the early 1830s, at St. Michael on the coast and at Nulato on the Yukon. Then in 1854 they built a mission halfway between, establishing a base in the region for more effective teaching and conversion. This site became known simply as Russian Mission.

Though Alaska was sold to the United States in 1867, Russian influence remains to this day. Many Russian words, such as those for butter and milk, have become incorporated into the Yup'ik language. As a legacy from the first Russian explorations, the Yup'iks still refer to white people as *kass'aqs*, from the word cossack. The Russian church suffered during the early years after the sale, but it survived the incursion of the Moravian and Roman Catholic missions that followed and developed in its own path throughout the cold war years. A unique tradition survives in some villages in the celebration of Russian Orthodox Christmas. *Selaviq*, as it is called, is a festival of food, singing, and prayer that continues almost nonstop for ten days and nights after January 7.

By the time of Alaska's sale to the United States, the Yukon River had become a thoroughfare into the interior for prospectors. The Alaska Commercial Co., an American business, had placed traders on the Kuskokwim at the Kolmakovskiy Redoubt site. They had also built a trading post about 150 miles downriver, across from the village of *mamterillermiut* ("people of many fish caches").

In 1884 Sheldon Jackson, a Presbyterian missionary and later a federal agent and Alaska's first Superintendent of Schools, asked churches in the United States to help in his crusade to bring better conditions to Alaska Natives. Jackson's vision included not just the claiming of souls but also economic and educational betterment, as well as the institution of western language and culture. The Moravians responded by establishing a mission in 1885 near the *mamterillermiut* trading post. They named it Bethel. The Catholics chose the lower Yukon region and built a mission at Holy Cross in 1888. They placed two missionaries on Nelson Island the following year.

The early missionaries found a people with a rich culture whose complex system of beliefs and ceremonies linked its members to the natural world around them. Masks, hunting implements, wood bowls, and numerous other articles were carved with images of game and spiritually allied beings. The Yup'iks believed they were just one form of life among other living things of equal respectability. All things had souls and these souls existed in a state of reciprocity with one another. Animals were believed to offer themselves to worthy persons and worthiness was measured in terms of respect for the spirits of the game. Shamans in the villages provided access to the supernatural world and gave guidance as to how the people were to negotiate their relationship with the natural world. Young people were taught rituals designed to ensure that souls re-entered this world from the supernatural one. Right thinking and action depended on this worldview, which placed humans as equals to all other things. Rituals ranged from small personal acts in the hunting and preparing of game or fish to the elaborate ceremonies observed by whole villages. Human souls, being part of the animal world, were no exception. The dead were treated with great care to be sure their souls remained awake and could leave the body at the proper time and in the proper way. The souls of seals were returned to the sea in the annual bladder festival. The souls of people were returned to earth in the naming of infants after deceased persons.

The Yup'iks lived a seminomadic life with small family groups traveling to hunting and fishing camps during the spring, summer, and fall. During the winter months these groups gathered in home villages and reaffirmed the community by means of celebrations. Ceremonies and dances for a variety of purposes took place throughout the year, but the larger ones usually were held in the winter when cold weather curtailed many other activities.

Varying in size from just a few families to over a hundred people, the villages were organized around a large central structure, the men's house or qasgiq, which was half dug into the tundra. The men's house provided an eating, sleeping, bathing, and work space for men of all ages. Women and children lived in small sod huts with food caches nearby on stilts out of reach of animals.

The men did the more arduous fishing and hunting of large game, often with hunting partners. Long hours were spent fashioning and repairing the needed equipment. At a young age boys moved to the men's house and were introduced to the close fraternity of men. The women gathered berries and greens and provided some of the meat as well. They set snares and fished, preserved and prepared the food, provided skin clothing and boots, and took care of the children. Some activities, like egging or an annual duck drive, were enjoyed by everyone, young and old, male and female. Marriages were made within community groups.

When the missionaries moved in they made many changes. Many set about to ban the ceremonies and festivals which they saw as heathen. Wishing to solidify families, they demanded that parents and children live together the whole year and not just at camps. These demands met only limited success until the advent of the devastating measles epidemic that swept the area at the turn of the century. Village groups were so decimated that the system of marrying within the group began to break down as families were forced to realign into new villages. By the 1920s, these population groups began to coalesce around missions and trading posts (Fienup-Riordan 1984). Churches were built and the men's houses were removed. The last one was gone by 1930.

The missionaries brought new technologies and alternative forms of health care. Well-fed and vaccinated, they seemed miraculously to survive the epidemics that swept through the region, an achievement that engendered both resentment and admiration. Some learned the language. They traded in goods and participated in traditional doings, although they sometimes didn't recognize the cultural significance of their actions.

By the 1890s exposure to western values, technology, education, and medicine had begun in earnest. In the latter 1800s prospectors and traders traveling on the Yukon had filtered through the area on their way to interior Alaska and Canada. After gold was discovered at Dawson City in 1896, there was a great increase of sternwheeler traffic as fortune seekers from the south traveled to and from the gold fields. Trading posts were established along the way. In 1899 the stampeders rushed down the Yukon from Dawson City on their way to the beaches of Nome. Later they filtered back inland in search of mines.

Gold was discovered in the Innoko River in 1906 and the communities of Flat and Iditarod were established there, just northeast of the Yup'iks' region. The two communities were supplied by shipping on both the Yukon and Kuskokwim rivers. Traders and villagers along the rivers were contracted by shipping companies to cut thousands of cords of wood to fuel the sternwheelers. This demand provided work along the river to a work force that was just beginning to feel the need for money.

By 1911 a winter trail was opened from Seward to Nome passing through Iditarod. For the first time, people and mail could move through western Alaska during the winter. Later, mail was mushed by dog team on a connecting trail to Bethel. It wasn't until 1926 that the first plane landed in Bethel, an event remembered by elders in the community to this day. Airplanes revolutionized travel in and out of rural Alaska.

A curious aside to this history is the introduction of reindeer to the delta. Sheldon Jackson instigated the project to improve the food supply for Natives in rural Alaska. Lapp herders from Scandinavia were promised a new life in a great land and were brought to Alaska to teach herding. Their herds came with them. The first Lapp family arrived in Bethel with its herd in 1901. By the 1920s the region supported the largest reindeer population in Alaska and was considered to be the best reindeer range in the world. But herding, the existing subsistence patterns, and a growing wolf population didn't mix. Political conflict over how the herds were to be administered and by whom contributed to the demise of the project. By the 1940s, most of the reindeer were gone, though a small herd is maintained on Nunivak Island. Some of the Lapps (known among themselves as Sami) married into village families, but little is left of Sami culture. The Lapp names still remain in some villages, however, and old men who learned herding still talk about their reindeer-chasing days. On any warm summer evening almost anywhere on the delta, school-age children can be seen playing Lappball, a Sami bat and ball game.

The establishment of schools was an important part of Sheldon Jackson's vision. The Catholics built a school and orphanage at the mission of Akulurak near the south mouth of the Yukon and another at Holy Cross. The Moravians had a school at Bethel and lobbied the government to establish schools in other villages. Because families were seminomadic and because of the vast cultural differences, parents were reluctant to send their children to the early schools. Such simple conflicts as whether children's hair should remain long or be shorn in order for them to stay healthy prevented attendance. Sadly, the devastating epidemics furnished the mission boarding schools with orphans. In 1925 the Moravians built an orphanage school near Kwethluk that remained open until 1973. As villagers gradually spent longer periods of the year near the missions and came to trust the missionaries more, the schools grew in importance.

A two-tiered system developed. The "native schools," funded by the federal government, were for Yup'ik children. The territorial schools were for white children and some of the more assimilated children "of mixed blood." Although this resulted in segregation in some places, such as Bethel, it mostly meant that all the children in a given village went to whichever school was available, if they went at all. The native schools eventually became part of the Bureau of Indian Affairs system, which was supposed to serve a variety of purposes including social services and health.

In the 1950s the Bureau of Indian Affairs began flying students out of the region to attend high schools in the Lower 48 states and in Sitka. I have been told that sometimes near the end of summer a plane would land at a village, and a man would climb out with a clipboard and start reading off names. Students would scurry around, given just minutes to pack their things before boarding. They would be gone for nine months.

A regional boarding school was opened in Bethel in 1972 but the parents continued to express their concern that their young adults were not at home during a crucial period in their lives, a time when the boys are taught the skills of hunting and girls learn to preserve and prepare food. A lawsuit was pressed by the Hootch family in Emmonak, leading to the state's construction of high schools in villages beginning in 1976. Now even the smallest villages have high schools.

From the early 1970s until the mid-1980s the Bureau of Indian Affairs gradually relinquished control of village schools to the state system, which had run the "white" schools in larger communities since statehood in 1959. At present there is one state-operated public school system divided into districts of varying size, and grades one through twelve are now offered in every village. Although the transition of teenagers back into the villages after so many years has not been easy, there is now a new interest among young people in traditional dance and other activities, which has given new hope to the area in its effort to maintain its traditional identity. Parents are still struggling to gain the influence they need over their children's education. They try to determine how the schools should best prepare their children for the ever changing future and also incorporate the knowledge of the elders into the curriculum.

The gathering of subsistence food, however, remains an essential, underlying theme of the current culture. Though outboards, snowmachines, and CB radios are used, it is only because food can more easily and safely be procured with these means. Yup'iks, faced by the demands of a difficult climate where hunger is never far away, have always been pragmatic and technologically adaptable.

A large proportion of the Yup'iks' diet is meat, fish, and fowl, foods that can be harvested locally. Many items in the American diet, such as milk products, fruits, vegetables, and grains are expensive and difficult to obtain. Surveys completed in the mid 1980s by the Alaska Department of Fish and Game in nine villages in the delta, show that villagers were harvesting an average of 700 pounds of wild food per person a year. At the same time the mean consumption of store-bought meat, poultry, and fish by Americans was 222 pounds a year (Nickerson 1989:14). Of the 700 pounds, 518 were fish, 75 were land mammals, 66 were sea mammals and 41 were other harvests such as greens, waterfowl, and berries (Wolfe and Walker 1987:63–64). Before the acquisition of snowmachines in the 1960s, families had to harvest an additional few thousand pounds of fish to feed their dog teams.

These figures represent a tremendous ongoing effort. Agnes Kelly Bostrom puts it this way. "All through the year we are getting ready, getting ready for fishing, for berry picking, for potlatches, getting ready for winter. We are always getting ready to go somewhere to get foods." This sense of constant preparation may come from the fact that subsistence activities depend on being ready at the exact moment that the conditions are right and from the fact that the right moment is unpredictable. She goes on to say, "And because we are so religious, you know, we are always getting ready for the next life."

Technology for subsistence has changed in recent decades. What has not changed is the spiritual connection between man and the animal world which is born out of intimate knowledge and dependence. Ritual distribution is still practiced, with game given to the proper relatives depending on the occasion. Parties are given to honor young boys and girls at the occasion of their first catch or berry picking. These observances are carried out with much ado and ethnic pride. Others, such as the correct handling of game or proper Yup'ik table manners, are quietly automatic, even unconscious.

At the same time, the churches are central to Yup'ik community life and to spiritual life as well. The three main churches—Catholic, Moravian, and Russian Orthodox (the church is now simply called Orthodox)—have Yup'ik deacons, priests, and helpers to help preside over the spiritual life of the village. A young person in some villages may be given both a communion party and a potlatch (a traditional gift exchange). Parents may name their newborn so that the child receives the soul of the grandparent and the name will then be recorded and blessed at a baptism. Bible study brings the old people together and provides them with the venue for instructing the young as they have always done. Church collections are used to redistribute resources to needy villagers in a way similar to redistributions at potlatches. This spirit has extended easily into church support for missionary work in other parts of the world. The women in one village knit blankets to be sent to children in Latin America.

A generation or two ago Yup'iks had all the skills needed to provide food, shelter, and clothing for survival on the tundra. Many of those skills are disappearing now. They are being replaced by newly needed ones: the ability to make enough money to buy heating oil and such things as outboard motors, snowmachines, and guns for more safe and efficient access to subsistence resources. The Yup'iks are also learning the skills necessary to negotiate regulations and advocate for conservation and management of the resources.

As artifacts in the museums show, Eskimo people have always been fascinated with technology and the development of efficient and specialized tools for living. As part of this tradition, people in the delta are open to the latest technologies, the improvements in communication, transportation, and health care that make the difficult and often dangerous subsistence life a little easier and safer.

However, traditional beliefs dictate that Yup'iks be deeply

cautious about any manmade changes that might have an effect on the productivity of the land and waters. It is enough that capricious natural events affect their food supplies. In testimony offered to the Bureau of Land Management in 1975, Peter Seton of Hooper Bay suggests how vulnerable his people feel: "It has been our concern for many years that it is not good to destroy our food potential. When any kind of waste spills or drains into our rivers, the fish will be destroyed thus destroying our main food supply. Even when there is a natural disturbance on the land there always seems to be a great reduction in the fish and wildlife around the area of that disturbance" (Nunam Kitlusisti 1976:6).

The late 1960s and 1970s brought a new consciousness to the area. In 1968 a public radio and television station began broadcasting from Bethel. The station was heard over most of the delta and was powerfully influential in that the people began to see themselves as a unified social and political entity. The Alaska Native Land Claims Settlement Act passed by Congress in 1971, as well as the Hootch family's successful suit to get high schools, also increased political confidence in the region. Opportunities for travel and economic development brought about by state revenues from the oil pipeline also contributed to the surge of regional identity.

The Land Claims Settlement Act attempted to resolve disputes between Alaska Natives, the state of Alaska, and the oil companies over land ownership. Under the Act, Alaska Natives relinquished claims based on aboriginal rights and received title to 44 million acres of land and $962.5 million. Native people became shareholders in thirteen regional corporations created by the Act and in newly organized village corporations. Calista is the corporation most Yukon-Kuskokwim natives hold shares in. Calista and the village corporations each received portions of the funds and title to specific lands. In addition a nonprofit arm of Calista was established in Bethel to address health needs of the region. The corporations were to run like any others, with elected boards, paid management, and, by 1991, the possibility of selling shares to anyone wanting to buy. The Yup'iks have

struggled to learn the skills needed to serve on boards, manage their corporation businesses, and deal with government requirements. Perhaps most importantly, the Act has defined them as owners and stewards of the land, roles which run directly counter to their conception of who they are as humans in relation to the natural world.

In the last decade there have been growing concerns about the long-term impact of the Settlement Act. Questions about buyouts, potential loss of the land to creditors, and about what will happen as Yup'iks are divided by their year of birth into shareholders and non-shareholders have come to light. One response, known as the sovereignty movement, has been an attempt by several villages to seek self-determination under a 1936 federal law, the Indian Reorganization Act. Under this plan, these villages hope to retain future control of their lands in spite of the Settlement Act. In addition they strive for Native control over such services as schools, child protection, and law enforcement. This conflict over what form governance should take typifies the complex issues currently faced by the region.

Even on a day-to-day level, life on the delta is full of difficult choices and conspicuous contrasts. In 1975 when I was working for the public broadcasting station in Bethel, most of the villages received their first telephone. We did a story on Toksook Bay on the day theirs were hooked up. John Active, the Yup'ik News director, called the village and a man's voice answered. John congratulated him in Yup'ik and the man responded that the village had now had the phone for twenty-four hours. He added that the weather was just fine that day, and that all the other men were out seal hunting. "But," he concluded in a wistful voice, "I have to sit here and answer this phone."

In Tununak in the spring of 1980 I attended a village movie. The room was packed. Many elders were sitting on the floor chewing snuff and spitting into cans while they watched *Psycho* II. A crowd of children swarmed outside, employing every possible means to get in. The adults preferred to keep them out not because of the content of the film (the movie is hardly more frightening than many traditional cautionary tales for children) but because they wanted to watch in peace. Today most village homes have VCRs and the most popular films are Kung Fu and horror films.

In 1983, at a fish camp below Mountain Village on the Yukon, sixty-three-year-old Louis George prepared a fire in the steambath. The steam house was the usual scrap wood construction about five feet high, equipped with a stove made from a fifty-five-gallon fuel drum. In case he might need more water or towels George brought in a VHF radio handset so he could call his wants to his family a few tents away.

Although Yup'iks today retain much of their ancestors' value system, they must contend with an unprecedented onslaught of change: mechanization, a cash economy, the Native corporation, land ownership, the pressure of outside interests on natural resources. They live in a culture in rapid evolution, with the excitement of new things affecting their lives every year. Just since I arrived in the Yukon-Kuskokwim Delta in 1973, many significant changes have occurred.

Television was introduced and now most villages receive many channels via satellite. Telephones were introduced, first as a single village phone and later in most homes. Health clinics with local paraprofessionals were established in each village. High schools were built in every village and government-funded housing was constructed in most. These projects brought an influx of outsiders, some of whom settled in the region, and this in turn brought small businesses, particularly to Bethel. A regional community college was founded.

These changes come at a cost that is hard to measure. Problems including suicide, domestic violence, and alcoholism are discouragingly prevalent. Non-Yup'iks and Yup'iks alike identify the connection between rapid cultural change and the serious social problems of the area and are often critical of the disruptions in lifestyle that have taken place. Many regret the passing of old ways while others point out that all cultures are dynamic. They argue that maintaining the trappings of the past and having a firm spiritual connection with it are not necessarily the same. It may not be the change itself so much as the speed of transition that causes such disorientation. The challenge faced by the people of the delta cannot be to resist all change but rather to resist changes that run counter to their spirit and to meet the future with confidence in who they are as a people.

Seals' Month, Kittiwakes' Season

Taqukat Tanqiat, Tengaurtet Tanqiat

Village of Toksook Bay.

Nelson Island hunters push through the ice toward open water.

Thomas Akerelrea, Scammon Bay, seal hunting.

SEALS' MONTH, KITTIWAKES' SEASON

Simeon and Paul John pull a bearded seal onto an ice pan, Nelson Island.

Prevented from seal hunting by ice conditions, Willie Hanson,

John Chikigak, and Richard Agayar, all from Alakanuk, fish for tomcod.

Successful seal hunters return home to Tununak.

Martina Phillip skins her husband Joe's seal, Alakanuk.

SEALS' MONTH, KITTIWAKES' SEASON

Clyde Smith and Curtis Augline take a break from bird hunting on the frozen Yukon River, Alakanuk.

Women of a Tununak family conduct a seal party, in which a young man's first bearded seal is distributed.

Blaise Tinker and Tom Tunutmoak in a firebath, Scammon Bay. The grass mouthpieces filter the smoke.

IN APRIL 1980 I TOOK THE MAILPLANE FROM Bethel 130 miles west to Nelson Island. It was a trip I had made many times. Departing at three in the afternoon, the Twin Otter was filled with cargo strapped into most of the cabin space with six seats for passengers in front. An older Yup'ik woman and I occupied the seat just behind the cockpit. She climbed in, took out her knitting, and seemed to observe nothing else during the whole hour-long trip. Bethel is just far enough inland from the Bering Sea that the moderating inland temperatures had melted much of the snow. As we flew toward the coast the snow increased until the ground was completely white except for the dark, curved, south-facing banks of the numerous lakes and rivers. Clear streaks blown off the surface of the lakes by the north winds added another texture to the tundra below. I had received a small grant from the Alaska State Council on the Arts to continue my documentation of village subsistence and I was returning to photograph spring seal hunting at Toksook Bay on Nelson Island.

On a map, Nelson Island doesn't stand out separately from the shore as does Nunivak Island, twenty miles farther west. But it is surrounded by water, with the Bering Sea to the west, Baird Inlet to the east, and two rivers that run north and south from the inlet to the sea. The inlet and rivers are so low that the tides pulse in and out. It seems an island more because it stands up surrounded by hundreds of square miles of utterly flat tundra and sea, a cluster of hills rising to a high plateau with 500-foot cliffs that plunge to the sea at the western cape. Five Yup'ik villages are referred to as the Nelson Island villages: Toksook Bay, Tununak, Nightmute, Newtok, and Chefornak, the last two are on the mainland just across the rivers.

Joseph Treca, a French Catholic priest, came to Tununak on the northwest side of the island in 1889 to establish a church there. He wrote in his awkward English that the "Indians are everywhere-Indians, and here principally they have their home where they have the food; therefore each season sees them transfer their penates [i.e., household] where is the fish, or where are the birds" (Treca 1890).

Dan Joe at Nightmute told me of growing up in the now abandoned village site of Cakcaaq, inland on the east side of the island. Inland villages have an advantage during the winter because they can easily get fish from the rivers when sea ice conditions make subsistence on the coast difficult and dangerous. People only came to the coast during the spring to hunt seal and later to harvest herring. So Father Treca and his fellow priest, arriving in August like so many clergy and traders during those years, established themselves at a summer camp and were surprised when many people moved in the fall to inland camps and villages.

In the middle of my flight, the copilot announced that although they usually land at Toksook Bay first, on this flight the cargo had been loaded in reverse so we would first land at Tununak, seven miles north. During our short stop there on the more exposed side of the island I noticed that the north wind buffeting the plane had filled the bay with fragments of ice. As we reached Toksook Bay I could see smooth sea ice, still intact and extending four miles out toward the open sea. Landing on the short field by the village, both pilots performed a flurry of hand movements on the pitch and throttle controls to thwart the attempts of the plane to lift in the headwinds.

I had visited Toksook Bay many times and Paul Agimuk, a short, stocky, graying man of about sixty, had often met me at the plane. By some unknown means he always seemed to know my flight. This time he wasn't there; he was playing bingo at the village hall where, as he later told me, he had won sixty dollars after spending only twenty. Over a cup of tea I asked him about the traditional movements from inland villages to coastal camps in the spring. He described how the village of Nightmute, about twenty miles inland up the Toksook River, would first move to a place on the southwest coast of Nelson Island called up'nerkillermiut, the Old Spring Camp. The coast on this side is made up of a series of gravel beaches at the foot of the bluffs that gradually rise from east to west. Up'nerkillermiut is on the last of these beaches. Beyond, the high cliffs of Cape Vancouver plunge directly into the sea.

The move from Nightmute was made with dog teams.

The dogs pulled sleds loaded with supplies and kayaks down the frozen river and across the smooth bay ice. The camp on the snowy beach, near the base of the 900-foot bluff, was close to the open water where kayaks could be used to hunt seals among the ice floes. When the ice melted, the village would move back five miles to Umkumiut, a fish camp that is still used. The herring spawn in May, and the camp provides a fine beach for drying the fish.

Paul said they often stayed well into August at Umkumiut before making the twenty-mile journey by boat back up the Toksook River to Nightmute. When the government built the school in the village the white teachers wanted the students to remain in school past the time of the usual spring move. This was a problem until the arrival of fast-moving snowmachines and outboards. The men could travel more quickly from the village to the seal hunting area, so up'nerkillermiut was abandoned. But in early summer, the move to Umkumiut was still necessary to catch and dry the many boatloads of fish required by each family. As people prepared to leave Nightmute each year, the teachers knew that many children would be taken out of school. One spring a teaching couple moved with the village to Umkumiut and finished up the school year in the fine little chapel there. But this was the exception and many families have had to work around or ignore the school calendar.

Dick Lawrence, a Toksook Bay elder, saw me photographing around the village and invited me in for some pancakes. He described earlier life in Nightmute and he talked about the move in 1964 when some of the younger families in Nightmute, which was on a rather crowded site, decided to form the new village of Toksook Bay.

"In Nightmute we lived in mud houses, sometimes three families together in a house twelve feet across, sometimes fifteen feet. We would build a fire for breakfast and heat up the house and then not have a fire all the rest of the day. We stayed comfortable. No sickness like there is now with everyone coming and going to the hospital. Five houses were moved down from Nightmute, small houses. Some of them were moved in the winter using dogs, eighty dogs

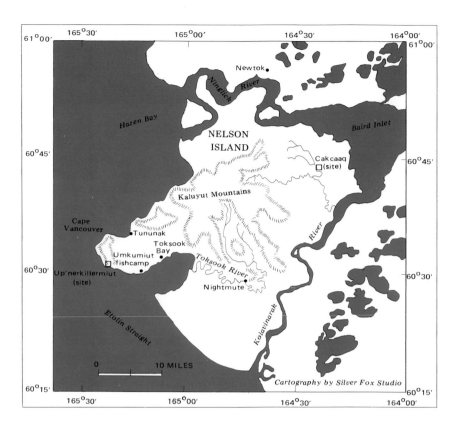

I believe. Others during the summer made a barge of oil drums and floated it out with the tides. We moved here because we could do everything from here—hunt seal, fish for herring—without having to move every spring.

"In the old days all travel during the summer was by kayak. There was only one large skin boat around here and one over at Tununak. In the spring when the move was made from Nightmute to spring camp and Umkumiut, two kayaks were lashed side by side together with poles to form a platform for carrying extra people and supplies. Travel that way was done only during calm weather. Not much stuff needed to be carried to the camps. . . . When we hunted by kayaks we went in pairs, two boats together, but many boats going out. Sometimes we would catch five seals, put them in the kayaks and paddle back to camp with the kayak very low. Water almost over the deck. Slow paddling! After seal hunting and the drying of herring, in the middle of the summer, we'd move back to the village. And then, get wood, driftwood for heat. All the time coming and going. I could paddle for many hours and not ever get tired."

The weather was stormy my first five days in Toksook, preventing the men from getting out in their boats for the spring's seal hunting. During this time, while the snow cover was still intact, the village decided to move a large diesel generator down to the shore where it could later be loaded onto a summer supply barge and sent out for repairs. It was on skids and some twenty young fellows were hired to move it. They first tried dragging it with ten snowmachines. They made a little progress, but the machines skidded and ended up facing in all directions. Ropes were then tied for hauling and long lines of people joined in to help. At the lead a teacher tied in her fifteen-dog team. The 7,200-pound generator slithered toward the shore in lurches, requiring frequent jacking to overcome obstacles. The chore was finally completed midafternoon. The tractor used for

clearing the airstrip wasn't working or it would have made an easy job of the task.

Eventually the storm front passed and the weather watch began. During the night people in Nightmute and Toksook Bay studied the weather trying to decide whether the following day would be suitable for hunting. There was much discussion on the CB radios throughout the evening and early morning. Paul John, who had offered to take me on the hunt, roused me at 4 A.M. I followed him over to his house and a warm plate of fried eggs was placed in front of me. The CB radio chattered in the background as hunters discussed the weather. The winds were near calm and the temperature was 10° F. The weak spring sun lit the landscape through an overcast layer of clouds. The Nightmute hunters would have to leave earlier than we would in order to travel the twenty additional miles by snowmachine to Umkumiut, where both villages' boats were stored.

Simeon John, Paul's twenty-one-year-old son, would be his father's partner in the hunt. Gear was loaded onto two wooden sleds behind the snowmachines. I rode in one of the sleds. Paul and Simeon joined the group of machines racing the four miles to Umkumiut on the smooth bay ice. I could see a curious darkness in the clouds ahead, a reflection of the darker open water beyond the white of the bay ice.

Umkumiut was a busy sight as the thirty boats were slid down the ice toward open water. Hunters stowed guns, CB radios, gas, tools, harpoons, tarps, food, and binoculars in the boats. Paul John's boat, an eighteen-foot aluminum Lund, was fitted with a 50-horse Evinrude. A 35-horse was laid crosswise on the floor as a backup. All of the boats from the two villages made an impressive fleet heading out to sea, but the hunt was soon delayed by ice blocking the mouth of the bay. Boats drove back and forth and the CB chattered during the search for an opening through the ice. After a while Paul John pulled up beside a grounded iceberg. Other boats tied alongside. Paul and another man climbed the fifteen feet to the summit and looked around, hoping to find an opening. There was no clear channel. Back in the boats Paul headed toward the old spring camp. I climbed the 300 feet up the

Gregory Strongheart, Scammon Bay, seal hunting.

bluff with the men who scanned the ice-blocked bay with their binoculars. One of the boats, a small speck from our high vantage point, was spotted working its way toward us through the ice. The boat stopped. A shot was fired, a faint "pop" in the distance. The men on the hill grinned and scrambled down to meet the boat as the hunters pulled the bearded seal ashore.

There seemed to be no other way to reach open water than by running boats up on the ice and dragging them across. Paul nudged the bow of his boat against the ice and raced the engine, and the boat literally jumped onto the ice. Paul and Simeon attached ropes and began dragging it the 100 yards to open water. Only a few years before, most of the boats had been wood, much heavier to drag across the ice. I walked along beside, pushing. I stepped back a couple paces from the sliding boat and grabbed a quick camera shot. Simeon looked back and with gentle understatement said, "Ah, better keep your hands on the boat." The ice wasn't solid.

When the line of sliding boats reached open water the hunt began. Each boat scurried off in a different direction and darted between chunks of ice. Now and again shots could be heard. Paul turned the CB off so he could attend to the hunt. Seals mingle among loose ice. The ice smoothes the ocean swells, making the boat a steadier platform for shooting accurately. Distant small black heads popped above the water. Paul and Simeon would carefully examine each with binoculars to discern whether it was a smaller seal or the larger bearded seal they hoped to bring home.

They spotted a bearded seal. Simeon positioned the harpoon in the front of the boat and pumped a round into the chamber of his 2-22 rifle. When Simeon was ready, Paul speeded the boat directly toward the seal. Simeon braced himself, locking his sight on the target. If the shot is fired from too far away the boat can't reach the seal in time to set the harpoon before the seal sinks. The seal didn't move. Curiosity held it as the boat rushed forward. Close in, Simeon fired. The bullet slammed into the splash of the quickly departing seal and Paul slowed the boat to an idle. Both men stood scanning the full compass around the boat, waiting

to see where the seal would pop up for air. A few minutes later, Paul spotted it and raced the boat forward. Four times he rushed the seal and Simeon fired. Finally, Simeon blurted, "Can't hit!" He unloaded the 2-22 and uncased a rifle with more punch, a 2-43 with a scope. At the next sighting Simeon's shot hit the seal. He quickly set the gun down and raised the harpoon. As Paul drove the boat abreast of the seal, Simeon thrust the harpoon into it.

The head of a harpoon is not permanently connected to the shaft but is tied to a long line that the hunter can hang on to if the seal swims or sinks. The harpoon head is curved and sharp at the tip and back edge so that it lodges itself firmly in the flesh of the animal when it is driven in. The shaft is then pulled free and the seal is secured by the line. Too heavy to be pulled into the boat, Simeon's seal could be towed to a spot where it could be dealt with.

Paul looked around, spotted a smooth pan of solid ice, and drove the boat onto it. Then both men heaved the 600-pound seal onto the ice. Smaller seals can be pulled directly into the boat from the water but bearded seals need to be gutted and skinned. After the heavy work of butchering, we all relaxed for a few minutes adrift on the small island of ice. The grays of sky, clouds, sea, and ice met at the horizon. We ate lunch in silence, both men dipping pieces of fresh seal liver into seal oil brought along for the occasion.

Later another bearded seal was dispatched with one shot from Simeon's 2-43. Two smaller seals were also shot and were pulled directly into the boat. By midafternoon Paul turned on the CB radio and listened as hunters began to assemble for the trip back to Umkumiut. In recent years the CB radio has provided an additional measure of safety for Eskimo hunters. When engines break down or ice conditions change, the CB is used to contact the village. Hunters chuckle as they tell about freak skips in CB transmissions. Sometimes when hunting they suddenly hear the voice of a truck driver down in Texas or California. They've occasionally held brief conversations with surprised truckers from their boats.

The men discussed their return route over the CB and

small groups of boats took off in different directions. It would have been impossible to pull the heavily loaded boats onto the ice, so the hunters needed to find an open lane back to the island. We sat for a while with a group of boats waiting for directions. Finally a circuitous route was found and the long line of boats snaked among the ice chunks. Nick Chanar and Larry John's boat was low in the water and traveling slowly, loaded with four bearded seal and a ringed seal. Paul John passed them a rope and took them under tow. With the heavy ice there was much concern for safety and the need to keep everyone together as the hunters threaded their way back to Umkumiut.

To ensure that everyone receives fresh food from the hunt, each village has traditional food sharing procedures. The practice differs from village to village, but usually the first *maklak* (bearded) seal taken each spring by a hunter is divided up and given away. The first seal taken by a young man is also distributed with a ceremony to recognize him as a new hunter in the community. After a seal is butchered, women are invited to the seal party. They bring buckets and other containers. A designated woman distributes portions of fresh meat or blubber to each bucket. This is usually the wife, mother, or grandmother of the hunter, or the mother of his namesake. Elders who no longer hunt receive generous amounts. All watch intently as the food is distributed.

Methods of seal hunting vary considerably from village to village depending on the proximity of each village to rivers and bays and the prevailing ice conditions. Seven miles north of Toksook Bay, on the other side of the island, the village of Tununak faces the sea to the north. There, as I had observed from the airplane, the north wind blows chunks of ice into the bay, thwarting boat launching. Tununak hunters will sometimes pull their lightweight aluminum boats by snowmachine across the island to the south, where they can hunt in better conditions.

I found seal hunting to be quite different north of Nelson Island. At the village of Alakanuk near the mouth of the Yukon, shorefast ice freezes to the land and extends out many miles into the sea. Hunters must travel great distances

over the ice to reach open water. There is no safe place to leave boats near the water's edge since the ice can break off, so the boats and gear must be sledded out to the edge of the ice for each hunt. Villagers from Alakanuk use very lightweight skiffs, about eight to ten feet long with no motor. These are easily loaded on sleds and pulled by snowmachines to the water's edge. The men hunt on foot from the edge of the shorefast ice. When a seal is shot the boat is quickly shoved into the water to retrieve it.

All during the spring of 1982, strong cold winds blew from the northwest and forced loose Bering Sea ice up against the shorefast ice. The Alakanuk hunters were thwarted. There was no open water near the edge, just a jumble of unstable ice. Since the open water is many miles distant from Alakanuk, it is important to be able to check from the village whether the conditions are suitable for hunting. Paul Tony of Alakanuk told how hunters judge ice conditions from many miles distant. "We look out our windows in the morning and see the reflection in the sky where the ice is." The land is utterly flat and white and any open water is practically black. The low overcast of the winter sky acts as a mirror and any dark area below can be seen traced in the clouds. Paul explained that the dark sea at the edge of the ice can be seen in the sky twenty miles away. "Right now, I can't see any line in the sky. That means with this north wind, that ice has been blown up against the shore ice where we hunt. Our hunting is blocked with ice. When the wind stops, the tides will move the ice out and it will be good hunting."

That April I went seal hunting from Alakanuk with Joe Phillip. Behind the snowmachine he pulled a sled loaded with his small aluminum boat. I rode standing on the back of the sled. We traveled the nine miles to the frozen shore and then ten more miles out on the ice. Reaching the edge of the solid ice we found ice fragments blown in and frozen in place. There was little open water and the ice pack was unsafe for further traveling. Joe did find one pond of open water about a hundred yards across. Kneeling behind a chunk of ice he scratched the butt of his rifle against the ice, a sound that entices the curious seal. One popped up. He shot the seal and quickly retrieved it. I later learned that this was the only seal Joe Phillip shot that spring because of the bad ice conditions. He usually gets nine for his family. That year there was a shortage of seal meat and seal oil in the lower Yukon villages. Other food sources had to be sought as a replacement.

A week later I again traveled with hunters to the same ice edge. The pond where Joe had caught his seal was frozen over. There was no open water visible. Wishing to retrieve something for their effort, everyone pulled out fish jigging gear, short sticks with lines and hooks. They chopped holes in the ice and spent the day fishing for tomcod. Each person caught fifty to a hundred pounds of fish for the day's work.

On my first few trips out onto shorefast ice, I wondered how travelers navigate on such a flat white plain. The trail had been well used by previous hunters and I did note that about five miles out it passed by a small ridge of ice about four feet high. This pressure ridge was caused by large sections of ice pressed against each other by currents. The trail stopped at the water's edge near another pressure ridge about twenty feet high. Other trails followed along the edge of the ice, branching from this mound. How did people find their way so far from the sight of land? Weeks later I posed this question to Matthew Beans, an older man from Mountain Village, upriver from Alakanuk. He said, "Did you see that big pressure ridge out there? Well, that's a shallow area and that pressure ridge forms there every year." Willy Duny, a younger man in Alakanuk, affirmed the importance of traditional knowledge for safe traveling. "I'm one of those smart Eskimos. I go out seal hunting at 9 A.M. a couple hours after the other hunters leave the village, and follow the tracks of older experienced men who know more about the ice than I do."

Norton Sound is a favored sea mammal hunting region for many villages located near the mouth of the Yukon. On October 6, 1981, the government held a hearing to find out what residents thought about potential oil exploration in Norton Sound. The villagers warned about the times when winds and tides drive the Norton Sound ice with devastating force and speed. In that testimony, recorded in Nunam Kitlusisti's summary publication in 1982, Phillip Foxie of Kotlik described his experience years earlier hunting by kayak:

"A friend and I went out hunting together in Norton Sound area. We got caught in the ice jam, the ice started moving very fast toward the shore. We couldn't paddle our kayaks fast enough to stay ahead of the ice even though we paddled as hard as we could. The ice caught up with us. My friend was lifted up on the ice. I was following him, sitting in my kayak on the ice as the ice rushed toward the shore. Then the ice on which we were sitting started jamming against the shore ice and I was lifted up. I reached out and grabbed the edge of the ice and held on as it tilted up. Then the ice broke and slammed down on the shore ice and I landed on my belly. I stood up, I tried to get to shore but the ice kept moving. We were almost crying from fear. Then the ice slowed down and we ran to the shore ice. When the ice jams like that it will go as high as fifty feet and sometimes higher" (Nunam Kitlusisti 1982:11).

Other villagers told how strong winds will "blow up the tides" causing serious flooding in flat regions. They described how in 1924 moving ice bulldozed fifteen miles inland, gouging the tundra and the permafrost beneath it and flooding many additional miles inland. Several families were caught in their camps by the onrush and were killed. When the waters withdrew, seals were left stranded far inland in lakes.

In spite of new technologies, seal hunting continues to be a risky undertaking. Wind and weather can quickly turn a successful hunt into a disaster. Back in the village, new stories are added to the old as the men recount the hunt and relax while the women skin and preserve the catch.

One April during seal hunting I went to Scammon Bay, a village on the coast south of the Yukon River. Blaise Tinker saw me walking around the village with my camera and invited me to have a firebath. "Bring your camera," he added.

Firebaths aren't used much anymore, although they were once the traditional means of bathing. An open fire would be kindled in the middle of the *qasgiq* or "men's house." This is

Leonard Raymond of Stebbins butchers a walrus.

a small structure dug partially into the tundra and made of driftwood timber and sod. The smoke goes up through · a hole in the ceiling. The firebath provides an intense dry heat and once it is ignited there isn't much that can be done to control the burn. The bath used today, introduced by the Russians, is the steambath. A stove, now made from a fifty-five-gallon drum, is placed in a small room. Hot rocks on the top of the stove are splashed with water, filling the room with exquisitely hot steam.

This, however, was a traditional firebath. The room was about ten feet in diameter, the sloping walls blackened with soot. The driftwood fire was ignited in a pit a couple of feet deep. Since it takes a couple of minutes for the chimney effect to clear the room, the *qasgiq* promptly filled with choking smoke. The five of us started coughing in the dense cloud. I was handed a smoke screen or "mask," a coil of grass tied together with a cloth, but I preferred a wet washcloth over my mouth. It seemed like a test to see how long one could stay inside a burning building. Fighting panic, I gauged my distance from the door and judged that I'd need one good breath to get past the person beside me. Suddenly the closeness of that smoke-filled room propelled me out of the door. There I was, midafternoon, standing naked in the snow in the middle of the village. Years later the village women kidded my wife about how they had seen me.

I went back inside when the smoke cleared. The smoke-filtered sunlight was shining into the room through the roof hole. The camera lens was badly steamed up. I kept wiping it, trying desperately to make it usable again. The room was quite dark and I had to estimate the distance. I took many photos and only the final frames were clear.

Two years later when I was taking a steambath in Alakanuk, Clem Joseph told me the following story about a large firebath on the other side of the river. "One time, when it was lit, it didn't give off much heat. A fellow was asked to put something on the fire. There was an old Sears catalog in there. He threw that on the fire. As each page caught fire the draft tore it loose and burning pages started flying around the room. The younger people danced and jumped around the room, cursing as the burning pages flew. Now we say, NO MORE CATALOGS IN THE FIREBATH HOUSE!"

Years before, I had talked with Betty Guy, a Kwethluk village health aide. She talked about steambaths. "Before, women did not take steambath—only men. Some women have arthritis. The doctors tell them to use steambaths. They started using steambaths—their pains feel better. Now, I have been using steambaths for two years."

For women, the work continues even after the seal meat is distributed. "Pokes" are fashioned out of whole skins turned inside out and filled with fat to be rendered. The oil, fresh or fermented, is a favorite additive to many foods. Hides are prepared and bundled away for later when long winter evenings will be spent making boots, parkas, and mitts. Every part of the seal is used.

One spring, on a warm sunny day with little wind, my wife Robin and I were walking around the village of Toksook Bay. There was the usual maze of clotheslines stretched from houses to poles, many adorned with drying clothes. Then we started noticing lines with no clothes, larger and fatter lines strung among the houses. On closer inspection it turned out that they were inflated seal gut hung out to dry. The almost weightless dried gut vibrated rapidly in the light breeze. The seal intestines had been carefully saved for weeks, waiting for the first warm, windless day when they could be safely dried. As I was photographing, Frances Usugan stepped out of her house and started bundling up one of the dried intestines. She paused in her doorway, amused, as I rushed over to photograph her.

Seal gut parkas are still worn by some hunters and women. The parkas are made by slitting the dried gut lengthwise, making a strip four or five inches wide and about fifty feet long. The women then use cotton thread and grass to sew the strip in a coil, making the trunk of the parka. The grass swells when wet, making the seam waterproof. I asked how effective they were in comparison with modern rain gear and was told that gut parkas are very warm, lightweight, pliable, and very dry. When wet they become more transparent, a thin membrane covering the wearer.

Frances Usugan holding dried seal gut, Toksook Bay.

Birds Have Young, Breakup

Irniviat Tengmiat, Cupvik

Spring flooding at Oscarville on the Kuskokwim River.

Melvin Tony, James Tony, and John Chikigak, all from Alakanuk, traveling on the Yukon.

Frank Woods hunting, Toksook Bay.

BIRDS HAVE YOUNG, BREAKUP

Frank Woods's family, Toksook Bay, hunting
birds and eggs in 1981, before hunting
at the time of egg laying was prohibited.

Mona and George Washington gathering firewood on the beach at Stewart Island near Stebbins.

BIRDS HAVE YOUNG, BREAKUP

ACH VILLAGE HAS A DIFFERENT PATTERN OF seasonal activities depending on the availability of game and the natural conditions. In the spring, villagers who live inland, up the big rivers, are as busy as the seal hunters on the coast. Upriver, everyone watches for signs of land mammals beginning to stir and birds returning with the warmer weather. Hunters travel to areas that have long been known to be good for spring hunting. In the past many families made trips such as the one described to me by a friend in Bethel, Carl Kawagley.

I came to know Carl in 1980 while we were both working as volunteers on the 300 miles of trail for the Kuskokwim 300, a new middle-distance dog sled race. A tall muscular man in his sixties, Carl was enthusiastic about reviving dog sledding and happy for an excuse to do the work involved. He and I traveled off the main trails in search of good routes and slashed through stands of willows creating new trails. Carl talked proudly of his work with dog teams during World War II. His group was assigned to rescue downed American pilots who had crashed while flying lend-lease planes from the Lower 48 to Fairbanks, where Russian pilots were to pick them up. In the National Guard after the war, his group of dog mushers were requested to experiment with cold weather gear and clothing. Chuckling, he explained that they would wear a particular kind of clothing one day during field maneuvers, then write reports describing the clothing's performance. The next day they would wear something different and write more reports. He thought some of the clothing ideas were pretty silly in comparison with the high standards of simplicity and serviceability long established by the Eskimos.

He liked to talk about growing up in the thirties with his family in Akiak, forty miles upriver from Bethel. One day at his home in Bethel I turned on the tape recorder and he told a story from his boyhood in the 1930s. It was about his family's annual spring trip, south into the mountains.

"When they see these snow birds starting to come around, they'd get ready to go. We'd take all the basics, the heavy stuff, and take it about thirty miles in a day by dogs. Then

go back. The next day we'd take the family up. Then we'd leave them there and then run the basic stuff up another thirty miles.

"My father would go with absolutely nothing. Before they'd leave the timber line, they'd look for spruce trees, maybe five to six inches thick, then split them, get everything ready and put it on the sled. We'd take it over to the place where we would build skin boats later on.

"We'd take one dog team, nine dogs. Before, they used to take only one or two dogs. That was in my grandfather's time. Nine is the most we can feed economically off the land.

"In the morning, I'd cut the fat off the belly of the beaver and just give the dogs a small portion. By God, when we'd start going—well, we'd have to repair the harness every evening! I'd be helping with the cooking and mending the harnesses. The more you treat dogs better, the more powerful they get.

"In them days, we had steel runners. But some of these guys would have ivory runners. Now, to cross a creek that had nothing but boulders and rocks, they'd cut a few branches of willows. They'd put them down, move the sled over. And when the sled passed, they'd move the branches over so the runners won't touch against rock until they get to snow again. These little things made us survive.

"Early April was the time we'd go. We'd take some dog salmon. Sometimes we don't even use that when we have enough from hunting. Once we get up there we'd start hunting. Then we'd get fresh meat, like beaver.

"The women would start setting the traps and get lots of squirrels, and they'd take care of the squirrel meat and take care of the squirrel furs. They'd hang them out, dry them, and dry the meat. The men would go out and get their beaver meat, their bear meat, their caribou.

"Each family had their own place to go. Our family was looking for the biggest squirrels and therefore we'd go the farthest. Some of these people would stop and start setting their traps and hunting, but our family always looked for bigger and better squirrels, over toward the Nushagak.

"All the time we're hunting for ptarmigan. Women would

set snares with linen. This linen thread, like nylon or something. First they'd rub it with a candle wax. You'd also have to wax the threads used for sewing skins of the boat together. They'd run the linen thread through the wax candles and it would waterproof the thread. They'd make a little fence and set the linen snares, and early in the morning the women would go out there and gather the ptarmigan caught in the snares. Everybody's hunting. Everybody's living off the land. We never run short of food.

"My aunt Alice, she'd set her traps. Well, you or I could only go around once during the day. But she'd be out all day checking those traps. She'd eat a little salmon for nourishment. If her snow shoes break down she'd fix them while she's checking her traps. She was resourceful.

"What you call buck brush, it's a long willow. During the winter the snow flattens them down. During the spring when the snow starts melting, this brush starts springing back up just as soon as the sun gets warm. My Dad always told me, when that brush starts springing up a little you'd better get the hell out of there and head back home.

"May 24 was the time my father would always start home, start from Nushagak side. I'll never forget it. There would still be lots of snow. We'd travel mostly at night when the snow gets hard. That's when you make lots of mileage. When we'd be traveling I'd look back to where we were just a couple days before and it'd be just a blue haze.

"We'd go to the head of the Kisaralik [River], where our ancestors, they'd make the skin boats, just below the lake. They'd assemble the framework and then they'd soak the skins and they'd start sewing the skins together. And they'd go out and get lots of grass, burn the grass, and then the tallow from the caribou would be mixed with the burned grass and it's just like tar. Then they lash the skins onto the frames and then they put this burned grass–tallow mixture on all the seams.

"It'd take four or five days to make the boat, at the most. If you have taken up reindeer skins, caribou skins, then you have to soak them, then they sew them. If we have to use skins that we just got, then we try to sun dry them as much as possible. In the sun, the skins get pretty hot. Then we take the skins back to where we're going to make a boat at the head of the Kisaralik, then soak them again after they dry them, sew them together.

"While the skins are soaking, they make a frame. When you make a frame, you have to have a bow. There is always a measurement. To me, it's about this high, up to the first ribs. You've got to make that bow, the height from the keel to the gunwale, so them two ends will meet. You put a rope, and you bring the two ends up like a bow, tighten up the rope attached to both ends of the ribs and bend them until they come up to your first rib. Makes a bow. After, the framework is done. They don't use nails. They'd lash them together. And those lashes are wet, and they pull them tight.

"The boat would be about twenty feet long, big enough to carry everything—dogs, whole family, pelts, sled, every-

Carl Kawagley, Bethel.

thing. Of course the pelts and skins would be put in a water-proof container. We'd put our sleds in the bottom of the boat. Then we'd load everything, and dogs last, so the dog's feet don't puncture the skin of the boat. Women watch the kids and dogs—whack them if they make any noise.

"Other families would be up there at the same place making boats. Sometimes two families don't see each other for a month, and then they'd build boats and come down the river together.

"When we are traveling by families, just as soon as the day breaks everybody is eating or having coffee. Just as the sun comes up, everybody quietly gets in the boat. Them women, if one dog makes a little yelp, they smack him. Everything is quiet. You don't want to distract the man up forward who is the lookout.

"The man in the back is the boss, the man forward is just a lookout. You listen to the man in back. I was usually the man in front, who would direct around the rocks, the trees. The man in back is the boss and knows where that skin boat is going to go.

"I'd get bawled out lots of times because when we'd start passing a brown bear, or some animal, I'd like to stare and watch them, and I'd get bawled out lots of times for not watching where we were going, particularly in a canyon. You travel quietly so you won't distract the front man or the back man, because they are concentrating on the river.

"When we start coming down, no hunting, none whatsoever. Every night we'd be so damn tired, but we'd always make a _maqi_ [steam bath], primitive, just like the Indians out in the States, I guess. They heat up rocks, and that loosens up your muscles, relaxes you for the next day's work.

"Everybody was healthy then. Gee, we'd come down from spring camp in the hills and we'd get to Akiak and we'd look at the people who stayed in Akiak and they'd look pale. I asked one of my uncles if he was sick all spring. 'Nope,' he said. All the rest of us were sunburned and weather-beaten—healthy."

Though few families go to spring camp these days because children are in school, the long sunlight still brings out those who enjoy subsistence. In April, women spend days at a time pike fishing, sitting at ice holes and visiting while they supervise small children and grandchildren too young to be stuck in school. One time Robin and I met our judge's wife, Margaret Cooke, at a party and noticed her deeply tanned face. "Have you been to Hawaii?" we asked. "No," she laughed, holding up her white hands, "just the Johnson River."

The Yup'iks have given their thirteen months names that vividly convey natural events or seasonal activities. Deep winter is _iralull'er_, meaning the bad moon, because it's so cold. After this comes _kanruyauciq_, which has to do with frost. Around March comes _nayirciq_, when seals are born. Spring arrives with _tengmiirvik_, when the geese come.

In the long, cold winter, people walk with heads down, pushing their way through the heaviness of the darker months. The returning long light of spring inspires faces to turn up again. Eyes, turned upward, search for the first cranes, then ducks, geese, and swans. By mid-March family funds and village stores run low and the remaining dryfish have a moldy tang that closes the throat. The arrival of the migratory birds signals spring and a welcome change from the winter diet.

Clyde Smith of Alakanuk took me hunting down the Yukon and talked about learning to hunt. He said that his father started teaching him how to hunt when he was seven. He first learned to shoot little birds because their sharper turns and darting flight helped sharpen his gun handling skills. His father taught him to hunt selectively, not to shoot at everything. Clyde remarked that other fellows go out hunting with a box of shells and blow them all away and bring home little. He added that birds are best hunted when you can act as if you don't really need them. They seem to come closer to an "uninterested" hunter.

Edward Aloysius is another Alakanuk hunter. He and a friend were once on a hunting trip to the south in the Black River area. He explained that the birds there fly low, too low to see them coming, making it difficult to get good shots. He said that as the birds continue north they fly higher over the more populated Yukon River. On this particular trip

Edward and his friend broke a shear pin in their outboard and were stranded without transportation. They ran out of food and had only a little salt, one match, and one shotgun shell. He described how he crept up very carefully on some ducks, even crawling through ponds of water in his determination to get food. Every time the birds looked up he'd stop, then he'd crawl closer and closer. Finally, when he was close enough, he fired his one shot and killed nine ducks. They built a fire of willows and kept it going for a week until a boat came. Meanwhile, his friend ran out of cigarettes, so he got some dried willow leaves and rolled them up in cigarette papers. He took two puffs and gasped that they were a little strong. When they were finally rescued he and his friend were given cigarettes. After only a couple of puffs the world started spinning around and, as he said, they both lay down and waited "until the bushes stopped moving."

Felton Woods hunts with a slingshot, Toksook Bay.

Gordon Westlock, an older man who grew up on the Black River in New Knockhock, a settlement that exists no longer, told me on tape about spring hunting with his father. "Lots of times my dad is going out. And I'd cry because I wanted to go with him. I was around seven or eight, something like that. He'd put me in the kayak, face backways, and I'd have so much fun hunting. Sometimes I'd fall asleep and he'd go up along the side of the lake, put me inside the kayak, in behind, and continue his hunting. It was warm in there. Sometimes I used to wake up and I used to see him catch loons, sometimes muskrat, ducks. We'd camp overnight. The people in our home would never be worried about us because the older people would say, 'Oh, that guy never come home— I guess he's catching lots of game. We're not worried about him.' But today when somebody never come home they gotta go search party. Those days when I was small we'd go out and they'd never search, they know he's catching so many."

Bird hunting on the Yukon-Kuskokwim Delta was made illegal for most of the year under the 1918 Migratory Bird Treaty Act. It is only legal to hunt migratory birds when they have left the delta in the fall. Since the earliest days of regulation there has been confusion and ambivalence on the part of villagers as well as enforcement personnel over what hunting should be allowed. Regulating hunting activities in the area has become very complex as villagers come into greater contact with the rest of the world and as pressure on wildlife increases everywhere. In general, Yup'iks are law-abiding to the letter, but the migratory bird hunting law runs counter to survival for many families and, more than any other regulation, disrupts the traditional flow of subsistence.

One time in the seventies I was traveling by small skiff along the coast and I arrived unannounced at the remote village of Newtok. The teacher, who was spending her summer there, met me at the dock and kept me talking for some time. Years later I was told that because of the type of skiff I was using the village was certain I must be a Fish and Game person. Villagers had asked the teacher to detain me on the dock until they could hide their birds. The teacher

gave the all clear signal when she found I was not an
enforcement officer, and everyone relaxed.

More recently, villagers have become aware of worldwide
conservation issues and have become more connected to
the political process. With the help of the federal Fish and
Wildlife Service, village representatives have worked with
the Alaska and California Departments of Fish and Game
to plan for the protection of species that are threatened.
This became the 1985 Yukon-Kuskokwim Delta Goose
Management Plan.

The grand finale of spring in rural Alaska is "breakup."
The weather warms up more quickly in the interior of the
state than in the coastal regions. The warmed, rapidly flowing water from the interior erodes the ice downriver until
the pressure breaks up the ice and pushes it downstream. At
Bethel, on the Kuskokwim River, breakup occurs about May
14, on the average, but it may be as early as the end of April
or as late as the first week of June. Five hundred miles
upstream from Bethel at McGrath, breakup happens about
two weeks earlier. The Yukon River breaks up about a week
later than the Kuskokwim.

Some years the ice is particularly thick. This can happen
if there are unusually long periods of cold weather when
the ice is not insulated by thick snow cover. This ice will not
break up easily. Water rushes downriver carrying pieces of
ice that jam against the unbroken ice, creating a dam. The
water backs up behind these ice dams and causes flooding.
In the delta region most villages are placed right on the
banks of the rivers so that families can manage the heavy
hauling from house to boat and back again that subsistence
activities require. The trade-off is that in some years they
flood. Villagers try whenever possible to build on the highest
ground near the water and in many places enough houses
are above the rising water so the people have a refuge. The
problem of flooding becomes serious in places such as the
lower Yukon where all the land is low. Huge areas are flooded
and currents can carry heavy ice pans through villages. As the
flood waters rise, families move out of low-lying homes into
schools, or they are evacuated by National Guard helicopters.

Boys with birds, Nightmute.

One spring when the floods were particularly high, my wife happened to meet a school chum from the East Coast who had flown in to Bethel with the Red Cross. He was a specialist in postdisaster trauma, having worked in refugee camps and earthquake zones around the world. That day he had been on several helicopter flights to villages where flood waters covered the ground and lapped at the sides of the houses. He described how people were sitting in boats waiting out the flood, watching the water fill up their homes. Shaking his head, he added that he couldn't understand why no one seemed upset. Some people were even cheerful! He had no way of understanding that Yup'iks are not likely to waste energy raging against natural events. More specifically he couldn't appreciate that no matter what the damage, breakup also means the end of winter.

The world is suddenly transformed. For weeks thin ice in the rivers and sloughs has made travel unsafe. Tundra snow-machine trails have been bare and wet. After breakup, the rivers are clear for boats. Families can scatter to fish camps where even the sun has no schedule. Summer truly begins the day the ice goes out.

In the spring of 1982 I was doing documentary work in Alakanuk, near the mouth of the Yukon, and I arrived in time for the flood. The flight from Bethel showed that the river was open for eighty miles up near St. Mary's and Mountain Village, but the current appeared to be slack. The water was rising at Mountain Village. We could see open water on the river down to about the head of the passes where the delta begins. The ice further down appeared solid, with the thick ice in the main channel remaining intact. When I arrived in the village I found everyone concerned and interested in whatever information they could get about the ice.

John Hanson, an experienced observer of the river, had inspected the ice on a flight the previous day and said that it looked quite solid and might jam up and cause flooding. The water level on the Alakanuk Slough (the channel flowing by the village) was dropping slowly, with the water dammed upstream.

In the village, all serviceable snowmachines had been

placed at least four feet high on steambaths or on top of food caches. Grounds around the houses were cleaned up, with all usable items placed high for protection. Firewood logs were tied down. Most homes had boats tied near the door. At least one boat had a tent constructed, ready for lengthy occupation. People talked about previous floods where they were forced to stay for as long as three days in their boats, tied up to bushes near their flooded homes. I was told that some men were napping during the day so that they could stay up at night to watch the river.

The following morning Terry Cook, the city manager, flew over the river with John Hanson. They reported that the ice remained solid down the Yukon four miles below Alakanuk Slough. The ice jam had shifted down toward the village of Emmonak, about fifteen miles upriver, with water rising at Mountain Village and Pilot Station. Water was reported to be running over the banks and spreading south toward the Black River. The pilot dropped food to a family stranded at a fish camp. That morning the river at Alakanuk rose one foot in twenty-four hours. Everyone knew that the river could rise very rapidly if the ice dam should break.

The river watch continued through the night and into the following morning. The anxiety about flooding had been building up for weeks, ever since Fort Yukon flooded a thousand miles up the river. At 8 A.M. the CB radios reported from Emmonak that the ice jam was moving and we could expect rapidly rising water. By 10 A.M. the river began flowing over the low bank near the village power plant. At 11:30 another flight reported that the jam had cleared out upriver and, much to everyone's surprise, the ice downriver that had seemed solid the previous day was now open, with clear channels running to the ocean. The slow buildup of anxiety was suddenly over.

Most people were relieved, but at the same time they felt cheated out of a little excitement. They would like to have had just enough of a flood to cover the ground and clear out the trash, just enough water for a family picnic in the boat, with the dogs barking from the roofs of their doghouses.

Immediately after the threat of flooding was over, activity

in the village took on a new focus—logging. During the early afternoon the men helped each other slide the boats that had been tied near their front doors down to the river. They then began preparations for roping logs out of the river. By 6 or 7 P.M. the first logs were spotted and the race began.

The delta region is treeless tundra, but in the interior of the state the Yukon and Kuskokwim wind through hundreds of miles of heavily forested land. As breakup swells the rivers, huge blocks of ice gouge the banks and the trees fall into the water to be carried away with the ice. The rivers bring down tremendous amounts of wood. Villagers downstream take advantage of this momentary flood of timber. Newer homes are equipped with both oil heaters and wood stoves. Fuel oil costs more than two dollars a gallon, so the procurement of wood can greatly reduce family expenses.

The men ran their boats up to the mouth of Alakanuk Slough where it branches from the Yukon River. The river had shoved a large pan of ice aground, providing a lookout point for spotting logs as they swept down. The four boats were jumped up onto the ice. The passing logs were judged according to their type, size, and quality, and the flowing ice was studied to look for safe routes to the logs. The men watched for the white bark of birch, often rotten in the center but prized as the only hardwood available. Spruce is the only other choice of worth. Much cottonwood comes down but, as firewood, it just smokes and doesn't provide much heat. Spotting a good log, the men in the first boat pushed off and, two to a boat, they worked their way through the moving ice. While the driver kept an eye out for oncoming pans of ice that could batter the boat, the man in front hurriedly tied a rope around the log. Then the log was towed quickly back through the ice and tied to the willow brush along the shore. The work required considerable aggressiveness coupled with expert boat handling as the men maneuvered among battering pans of ice. The men worked late into the evening, some past midnight. Everyone knew that after the wood washed past for those few hours there would be no other easy opportunity to stockpile fire-

wood until the following year. From then on throughout the summer it would have to be searched out along the shores, pulled from the banks, made into rafts, and towed into Alakanuk Slough. Often life in rural Alaska can appear slow and relaxed, but opportunities for subsistence activities are fleeting and villagers then show impressive speed and determination.

A few villages are located on shorter rivers that don't originate in forested country. Three of these villages—Nunapitchuk, Kasigluk, and Atmauthluak—are located about twenty-five miles west of Bethel on the Johnson River where whitefish are available. They are referred to as the tundra villages. Teddy Brink of Nunapitchuk described how, in the 1920s before they had outboards, they moved logs upriver from the Kuskokwim to the village. The villagers brought their firewood to Nunachuk (the old village site near Nunapitchuk) after subsistence fishing was finished in the summer. The men would first paddle the thirty miles down the Johnson to the Kuskokwim, then up the Kuskokwim about sixty miles. Near Akiachak they would form rafts of logs and let the current carry them down to the mouth of the Johnson. Because the region is very flat, tidal action extends almost a hundred miles up the rivers. The men would use the tides to pole the rafts up the river in stages. It took two weeks to raft in enough logs to provide the year's supply for one or two families.

From pike fishing through the spring ice to wood gathering after the flood, the season offers a welcome round of activities out of the village. Robin and I once arrived in Scammon Bay at this time of the year. Coming up the hill from the airstrip, we encountered our friend Gemma Akerelrea and began to quiz her on the whereabouts of various people we hoped to contact. "Had she seen so-and-so? Was so-and-so in the village?" After having to say "no" to several inquiries, Gemma must have noted frustration in our faces. She shrugged and smiled, amused at our lack of observation and patience. "The spring is here and everyone is busy."

Smelt Running Season, Fish Hitting

Qusiirvik, Kaugun

Nightmute villagers' fish camp. Umkumiut, with houses and fish drying racks. The Catholic chapel is at left.

Phillip Foxie mending a salmon net, Kotlik.

John Helmick and Nicolai Evan
repairing an outboard engine, Kwethluk.

Hauling water from snow melt, Umkumiut.

John Joseph and Joe Lincoln pulling nets in bad weather, Toksook Bay.

Clifford and Bernie Tom pulling in a plugged herring net, St. Michael.

Sophie Amadeus covering fish,
Umkumiut fishcamp.

SMELT RUNNING SEASON, FISH HITTING

Louise Kanrilak braiding herring with grass, Tununak.

Wearing a seal gut parka, Jesse Paul from Kipnuk collects herring eggs deposited on seaweed, Nelson Island.

Herring on drying racks, Toksook Bay.

Ella Tulik taking down dried herring, Umkumiut fishcamp.

SMELT RUNNING SEASON, FISH HITTING

Clara Akagtak storing dried herring. Umkumiut fishcamp.

Simeon Tulik watches Sam Anthony
play Lappball, Umkumiut.

Pulling barrels of rendered seal oil to the boat, Umkumiut fishcamp.

Evening clouds over Nelson Island.

SMELT RUNNING SEASON, FISH HITTING

MOST OF THE VILLAGES ON THE YUKON-Kuskokwim Delta rely on salmon as their main food. But as salmon return each summer from the Bering Sea, they bypass the small tundra rivers and target the Yukon and Kuskokwim which lead far inland to rocky spawning grounds. Halfway between the mouths of these two great rivers lies Nelson Island. There, salmon are scarce, but the rocky shoreline of the island, covered with a healthy growth of seaweed, provides a rich spawning area for herring, which is the main fish for the Nelson Island villages.

In June 1976 Robin and I took a Twin Otter out to Nelson Island. We planned to land at Toksook Bay on the south side of the island and at low tide we would walk the four miles along the beach to the fish camp, Umkumiut, where the people of Nightmute come every summer to put up their year's supply of herring. Because of spring thaws the airfield was too soft for us to land at Toksook Bay, so we were let out at the village of Tununak on the north side of the island.

There I asked a friend, Andy Chikoyak, if he could give us a ride to Umkumiut around the western end of the island passing Cape Vancouver. The weather was fairly clear but there were winds kicking up some waves. He looked carefully at these conditions and even talked to some elders for further advice before we departed. Andy grew up in a flat tundra region somewhat inland from Tununak and above Baird Inlet. "I'm from a family of nomads," he once explained. "There were some years when we were low on foods, we know what it was like to be hungry. Now, any time I see food wasted I think back and remember. You don't forget hunger. . . . The most important stories passed down through our culture is the importance of not wasting food" (Nunam Kitlusisti 1981:7).

Andy is a talented filmmaker and painter. (He told me that his older brother used to use a folding still camera.) He once worked as an artist at the University of Alaska in Fairbanks, where he became friends with documentary filmmaker Lenny Kamerling, and helped Lenny make a film about Tununak. He later made his own film at Tununak,

Once Our Way, about the construction with drift logs and sod of a traditional *qasgiq,* a meeting house mostly used by the men or for ceremonial occasions. The film concluded with dance and the pounding of skin drums inside the log walls of the *qasgiq.*

As we traveled in Andy's skiff through Etolin Strait between Nelson Island and Nunivak Island, we skirted the cliffs of Cape Vancouver. The cliffs, which extended 800 feet above our heads, were covered with roosting puffins, auklets, arctic terns, gulls, and cormorants. Andy described methods the villagers used to gather eggs, greatly emphasizing his people's concern for the rookeries. I'm sure our expressions reflected his absolute earnestness but suddenly, with a glance at my photo equipment, there came a barely detectable gleam in his eye. With a smile he asked, "You want to see some birds fly?" He took up his rifle and directed where to point the camera. At the sound of the shot the cliff exploded in the breathtaking flight of thousands of birds.

Passing the old spring camp, we rounded the southwest corner of the island, and entered the quieter waters of Toksook Bay. Another five miles up the bay, we rounded a small point marked by a single rock standing about forty feet high. There in the next curve of beach was Umkumiut. A row of gas-powered Maytag wringer washers put-putted on the gravel beach. We had arrived on laundry day.

Andy led us up the beach, introduced us, and set off back to Tununak. We asked where we could pitch our tent and we were hesitantly directed to a fine tundra slope above the camp. We erected our small backpacking tent there but were not allowed to stay even one night in it. After getting a look at it (and at us, I imagine) the people decided that our tent wasn't adequate protection against the periodic stormy days. They graciously invited us to stay in the tiny cabin built for visiting priests. I stayed in that cabin during various visits a total of about five weeks, mostly during the summers of 1976 and 1979.

Umkumiut is one of the largest, most established fishcamps on the coast. It lies on a south-facing beach shielded from north winds by tundra-covered hills. Two enormous rocks at the western end of the crescent-shaped beach give the camp its name, which is possibly derived from the word "two." Two pieces of the point of land between Umkumiut and the next beach have separated and fallen towards the sea, making a shadowed gate to the west. Several people told us that long ago these rocks had fallen in order to crush several men, attackers from another village.

Umkumiut looked like a small village and everything was beautifully organized for the work that was done there, catching and drying herring. In from the beach were seven sets of large fish racks made from substantial drift logs. Farther back were eighteen small sheds used for storage. Behind these stood a row of fifteen cabins and a few tent frames. At the very back was an attractive, contemporary Catholic chapel, its design inspired no doubt by the beauty of the setting. In front of the drying racks, just where the driftwood was deposited by the sea, were half a dozen small, squat steambath huts.

We soon realized that the camp was inhabited almost entirely by women, children, and old men. Most of the village of Nightmute, about twenty miles inland, used to come to coastal camps on this part of the island in the spring to hunt seal and they would stay on at Umkumiut to catch and dry herring. Now, with fast snowmachines, seal hunters from Nightmute travel back to their village each day and no longer live at the camp. Also kids are kept in school at Nightmute through most of May, further shortening the time that families now stay at the camp. The men had been there for a few days to catch the herring and then had left for other summer work. Some had jobs back at the village but most worked on commercial salmon boats or in the canneries in the large Bristol Bay fishery to the south.

After the herring are put up, the camp seems to be on vacation. Everyone does a lot of visiting, and short trips are made to go after herring eggs, shellfish, and other delicacies. A species of smelt, called *cikaat* in Yup'ik, spawns along the shore, and villagers enjoy catching the small, oily fish by the tubful with dipnets. Women pick wild greens or grass for various uses. Alice Abraham, who spent childhood summers

in Umkumiut, said that once the fish were put up, the women used to busy themselves making fancy grass baskets for the annual arrival of the Bureau of Indian Affairs ship, the *North Star*. Until the advent of state-operated schools, the *North Star* plied the coast delivering fuel and supplies for the BIA schools and the villages. The women would either sell the baskets to workers on the ship or exchange them for newly arrived goods at the store.

One May morning I took a walk on the beach. The air was absolutely still, the waves inaudible. William Dull came toward me, carrying his finds from the beach—a load of small driftwood and a five-gallon bucket. I pointed toward Nunivak Island, saying I'd never seen the bluffs standing so visible or so high. He nodded in recognition of the mirage. Apparently this was a weather signal. He said that warm winds come from the southeast and cold winds from the southwest. He explained that when such mirages appear, the wind generally comes from their direction. "Maybe the winds will shift today." He said he had heard some boats leaving early this morning, perhaps to beat the weather change, "going out to get something to eat." Perhaps they would get mussels, clams, and other things. A few hours later, as he predicted, the wind shifted to the southwest, from Nunivak Island.

On our first visit in 1976 we had brought supplies but we lacked fresh vegetables. Robin found a solution to this problem. She discovered ferns just coming up near the stream and said they looked like smaller versions of the fiddleheads she used to eat in Vermont. She decided to cook them for supper if we could verify that they were edible. Since few of the women spoke much English this turned out to be problematic. Just before supper an old woman, probably in her seventies, stopped to watch as my wife rinsed the ferns in our pot. Robin pointed several times to the ferns and to her mouth, making questioning motions. The woman gave no response. Finally my wife pointed to the woman's mouth and back to the ferns, questioning again. There was a moment of recognition, a big smile, and the woman said, "*Quyana*" (thank you). She reached into the pot, popped a raw fern into her mouth, and walked away chewing, leaving us unsure as to whether the ferns were a delicacy or whether we might have poisoned her (well-mannered Yup'iks never refuse food that is offered). Just to be fair we went ahead and ate them, enjoying the fresh greens immensely.

Ignatius Mathias, one of the few younger men at Umkumiut in 1979, agreed with me when I remarked that one of the good things about the camp was the number of energetic old people. He spoke of how concerned he was that old people should remain in the village rather than be sent to the Pioneer Home in Anchorage. "People living at home can do the slightest things to keep physically healthy. If they quit they'll just fade away." He continued by saying how much he enjoyed having his mother live with them because she enjoys the children so much. "Spoils them rotten actually. Having many children is like having a life insurance policy. They'll take care of you when you get too old to do much."

At the west end of the beach is a stream of meltwater from a snow bank that lingers well into the summer. This water runs cold and clear over the gravel beach and into the bay almost directly under the two tall rocks. It is the children who must carry water from the stream to the cabins or wherever else it is needed. Often a group of two or three of them could be seen stepping lightly toward the stream carrying buckets, pails, and pots, sized according to the strength of each child. In a few minutes they would return struggling with their loads, some bent to one side against the weight of a single pail, others sharing the load of one large container. I've seen buckets arrive home with only a few scant inches in the bottom. Parents look at this performance with amusement and gently send them back for more.

One morning I heard a loud thump from the beach and noted a large wooden skiff departing loaded with people. A few minutes later I walked down and found a huddle of young fellows around an aluminum skiff. The passing wooden skiff had slammed into the starboard side, bending the gunwale. One of the boys explained that it should be straightened, "so my dad at Toksook Bay won't notice it." He went on to tell how the driver of the wooden boat had poor

vision on one side because a fish hook had once lodged in his eye. The ramming occurred on that side of the skiff. After trying to straighten the bend the fellows resorted to pounding the side with a large drift log. Again and again the log was slammed against the bent rail, until the boys were satisfied that it wouldn't be noticeable.

The average family will put up one or two tons of herring each spring, enough to last a whole year. After about three weeks, depending on the weather, the fish are taken down from the racks. To store the fish, some women make a rough, loosely woven basket that will allow air to circulate. Gunny sacks are also used. I watched Clara Akagtak sit for four hours with a pile of grass and make one of these tough utility baskets. I have seen women stand on the fish to stuff them inside and then quickly braid the top shut.

On one visit I watched Ella Tulik and her family load their boat to head back to Nightmute at the end of the herring season. Wearing rain pants as protection from the oil that oozed from the herring, she took down their partially dried fish. With a matronly hustle and authority she directed her sons in the transfer of the fish to the boat. At one point she flung a garland of fish five feet across the water into the waiting boat. Black clouds moved in from the east and there was just a hint of rain. At first she thought the boat was full enough but then, with a glance at the calm bay, she decided that more fish could be safely carried. Two more washtubs of fish were carried down. Enough! The load was covered with a tarp. She walked back to the cabins, talking briefly with a small group of women squatting there. They all laughed at something said. She teasingly threw a stick at them and hustled away. One of the women picked up the stick and tossed it at her retreating back. Without turning her head she dodged it—great laughter!

We knew that Umkumiut was not as busy a place as it had once been and we felt lucky to be there that first summer before too much had changed. Over the following years as the villagers bought bigger and faster outboards and boats, the men could get to the fishing grounds from Nightmute and families could tend the drying fish from home. Only two or three families now move to the camp. I asked why fish aren't taken back to dry at Nightmute and was told that it is too warm there away from the cooling sea breeze and that the fish would "cook."

There is much to learn about herring fishing, as I discovered in my trips to Nelson Island over the years. Herring arrive in the latter part of May or early June, but it was a trick to be there when the fish arrived and when the weather was right.

In mid-May of 1980 I put all my gear together and Robin and I flew out to Nightmute. We waited for several days as a guest of Father Dick Case in his one-room rectory. Father Case was the priest for the whole of Nelson Island, so he flew his Cessna from village to village. On the back of his mechanic's coveralls were embroidered the words, "Down-draft Dickie." He arrived soon after we did, just as bad weather closed in. He explained that he had just been to Toksook Bay where he had been summoned to bless the boats before the herring season. "I hope it works," he added.

Waiting is always harder if you don't know what to look for. After a few days I asked Dan Joe how we would know when the herring arrived. "You can tell when the herring come," he explained. "The herring gulls fly around and make lots of noise, and the herring are like oil on the water— the surface becomes smooth. Also the people start yelling a lot on the CB radios. Even if it's in the middle of the night I send my boys down to get them. They don't stay around long.

"You got to get up, you got to move around to get your food. You got to work hard. If you just stay in the village you won't get five cents."

Once I had seen herring come, I gained an appreciation for the furious work involved. As Joe Post of Tununak once explained, "The fish come in very fast, don't stay around long, maybe thirty-six hours. You have to get them quick. I got all I needed in three tides."

Herring arrive in three distinct groups; the oldest spawn first. Peter Dull of Nightmute explained that the first herring are very fat with oil and hard to dry. The later fish have less oil, which is preferred, but the fishermen catch some of the first ones in case the second don't come. These first fat ones are dried differently; they are slit in the middle, opened up, and laid out on a flat surface to dry. The second wave of fish are gutted and hung up. The third and youngest group are considered much too lean, having the texture of cardboard when dried.

Skiffs are used to set gill nets. If set in the right place, with the right tide, the nets may be full of herring in less than an hour's time. The midsection of the boat is often lined with a tarp, forming a bin to hold the fish. A full net is pulled a few feet at a time over the gunwale and shaken to remove the fish. It is then passed over the other side of the boat where it continues to catch fish.

Once in Toksook Bay Dick Lawrence told me about herring fishing by kayak. "We'd fish for herring using nets made of tendons from seal. The nets made by the women were twenty-five to thirty yards long. With kayaks we'd set them. Then when getting fish we'd pass the net over the front of the kayak. Pull the fish out one at a time and place them in grass baskets behind and in front of us in the kayak. Sometimes the women would make a grass mat, tied up at one end. We'd stick that mat way up inside the kayak. Then as the fish would pile up inside we'd kick them forward to make more room. On shore, we'd pull the mats out and all the fish would come. Back then we'd catch as many herring as we do now. It would take five to ten kayak loads going back and forth to shore." He added that, because the herring had to be caught in such great numbers, yet pulled from the net and gutted one at a time, the fish was nicknamed the "one-at-a-time fish."

Today, men do the fishing and carry their catch ashore in tubs. They are dumped into lined pits which are dug in the ground and covered with plywood or tarps. Here the fish soften for three to five days. When they are ready the women begin preparing them for drying. A woman may work at this for several hand-numbing days in miserable weather or, if the weather is sunny, it will be an opportunity to sit in the sun with other women talking, laughing, and working.

She takes the herring with the head in her left hand and opens it under the gills with her left thumb, gutting it with two quick strokes down the stomach with the right thumb. Fish eggs are separated from the fish and spread out to dry. Blades of rye grass, picked the previous fall when it was strong, are passed around the gills to braid the fish together. The resulting garlands of 70 to 100 fish are up to twelve feet long.

These garlands are hung over drying racks made from driftwood logs. If logs can't be found, then thinner poles are bound together in a teepee-like circle and the garlands of fish are draped around them. One older man pointed these out to me and referred to them with a smile as "skirts." Several times a day the garlands of fish are rotated, turning them over to dry evenly. Tarps and old sealskins are thrown over them if it begins to rain.

After a week in Nightmute, Robin and I went by boat to Toksook and took the mail flight over the island to Tununak. With the bad weather, Andy and Alice Chikoyak let us stay with them for a night or two. Gray clouds hung over the hills and the temperature was around fifty with wind and periodic rain. The beach in Tununak faces the cold north wind, but this was where the herring catch had to be prepared. The women had been working in the cold, hour after hour for several days when we arrived. It was too cold for Alice to bring her children, especially the baby, so Robin babysat for the day we were there. Andy and the other men brought hot coffee and adjusted the large pieces of plywood and tarps they had erected to provide windbreaks for the women. They tried to help by shifting the weighty tubs of fish as needed and by hanging the heavy garlands. Day after day, for as long as a week, Alice and the other women worked in the rain and wind until all the fish were up. Hard work is generally taken for granted in the villages. Everyone simply does what has to be done and only rarely is much appreciation overtly expressed.

Herring also spawn near Stebbins, a village seventy miles up the coast from the Yukon Delta. I talked with Walkie Charles from Emmonak, who was visiting there, and he told me about putting up his aunt's fish. "Me and a cousin, we've just finished doing herring. Our aunt's too old to work so we had to do all the fish. I never realized how much work it was. You know, going out and fishing and hunting is easy and fun. But we had to sit hour after hour, six hours one day, five another, gutting them and then stringing them up. It is so tiring. There I was sitting and working all those hours, thinking the same thoughts my mother would think when she was doing fish—well, it's incredible the amount of work these women do. I'll never eat fish again without thinking about all the work these women do."

One year I arrived at Toksook Bay just when the herring had started spawning. But arriving with me was a strong southern storm. Theresa Lincoln teased me about bringing bad weather for so many herring seasons. Storms at this crucial spawning period are feared by the Nelson Island villagers. I visited Larry John while we waited for a change in the weather. He remembered other years when the weather interfered with the catch. "One year there was a strong wind. We couldn't catch herring, but they were there. We caught lots of hooligans (smelt) and got through the year on those." Everyone was worried because a storm at the wrong time can prevent the harvest of the year's supply of protein. George Nevak seemed convinced that the worst had happened. "That southwind, it really hurt us," he said. "I don't think any more herring will come. Our fish racks are almost empty. We usually put up about a hundred loops of fish. Now we have only ten up. Yesterday we checked the net, only twenty to thirty fish. We kept them all, don't waste any except the ones eaten a little by birds. If we don't get any more by fall we'll have to hunt for walrus, go for tomcods. The herring is the only fish that comes here a lot. Sometimes in the winter some put nets under the ice up the Toksook River above Nightmute. Catch 'loche' fish (burbot or ling cod). Maybe ten to fifteen each week. That's over twenty miles away which is a long way to go."

Finally the spring storm abated. Fishermen went out and reset their nets. The catch was slow. The storm had disturbed the fish and they no longer moved in the usual mass, but the fishermen kept working their nets and eventually caught enough.

Even if fishing goes well, other factors can interfere. In 1989, after the hard work of catching and putting up a year's supply of herring, wet weather prevented the fish from drying. The whole harvest was lost to mold.

Over the past two decades Nelson Islanders have faced worries and decisions regarding the herring stocks. Hard choices had to be made as villagers weighed their fears about the survival of the herring against their need for money. Fluctuations in the herring returns, overharvest by uncontrolled foreign fleets in the mid-Bering Sea, and pressure from the domestic commercial fishery forced the villagers into the political arena. For the first time, Nelson Islanders felt vulnerable to the world's growing demand for food. They were fearful about the continuation of their essential yearly supply. Louise Kanrilak said simply, as she finished braiding a long garland of herring at Tununak, "Herring are very important to us. When we are out of herring, we are out of food."

At the same time people needed money. They were too far from the commercial salmon fisheries to have received the fishing permits that are now required for commercial fishing in the region. Although they worried about the impact of commercial herring fishing on their much-needed subsistence sources, the villagers recognized that regulations would eventually force commercial fishing in the area. They had no choice but to trust in the biologists' and the politicians' ability to manage the resource. After much discussion, they lobbied for regulations that made the fishery less appealing to commercial fishermen from outside the region. In 1985 the Alaska Board of Fisheries approved the regulations the villagers sought. With this, the villagers entered the commercial fishery using their small skiffs and subsistence gear. Gradually the men have upgraded their boats and equipment to make them more competitive.

In 1986 I visited Nelson Island to see how the subsistence and the new commercial fisheries were working together. The first group of fish that come ashore to spawn are the fish with the highest roe content and are targeted by commercial fishermen. These eggs, a great delicacy in Japan, are the primary product of the commercial herring fishery. For this reason the commercial harvest commenced first. When the fish arrived the Department of Fish and Game flew over the spawning grounds to estimate the tonnage and calculate the amount of fish that could be commercially harvested safely.

About a week after Fish and Game closed the commercial fishery, the second group of herring arrived. These are preferred for subsistence use by the islanders. I had noticed that the income from last year's commercial fishing had been put to use. Some fishermen had bought lumber the previous summer and during the winter they built themselves larger boats. With the additional income from the second season some planned to add motorized hydraulic rollers for pulling nets more efficiently. Present regulations help them to compete with the bigger, well-equipped boats from "Outside," but the villagers know that they need to increase their efficiency in order to cope with possible regulation changes.

As new technologies become available, villagers are able to go after food sources that weren't harvested in the past because they were not dependable. Halibut fishing has developed in a small way and even salmon can be gotten. In 1980 I noticed that Larry John, a particularly aggressive hunter and fisherman, was unloading a few king salmon from his boat, something I had not seen before in Toksook. "We really like them, both of us. An old man in the village said we would have lots of kings and reds this spring because the wind was blowing from the north for a month. So I bought an extra freezer just to keep the kings."

I suspected that when the wind blew from the north that spring some of the Yukon River water was pushed south and flowed along the coast past Nelson Island. King salmon sensed the river water in the Bering Sea and followed it. Larry had placed his king net out in Etolin Straits and he was catching kings, five to fifteen every day. His freezer quickly filled up and he gave many away. I heard that a few other fishermen were considering buying king salmon nets.

King Salmon

Taryaqviit

Salmon drying at the Hoover fishcamp near Bethel.

Charles Hanson salmon fishing
on the Yukon River, Alakanuk.

KING SALMON

Anesia Hoover gathering alder limbs
used to hold salmon fillets open for drying.

Cutting and drying salmon. Black River fishcamp.

KING SALMON

Joe Chief drying salmon, Bethel.

Katherine Uttereyuk putting the day's catch up to dry at Black River.

Repairing a salmon net, Black River fishcamp.

"Scare-gull" made of a *qaspeq* on a fish rack, Bethel.

KING SALMON

Pulling a beluga whale onto shore,

Black River fishcamp.

Mike Uttereyuk butchering beluga.

Black River fishcamp.

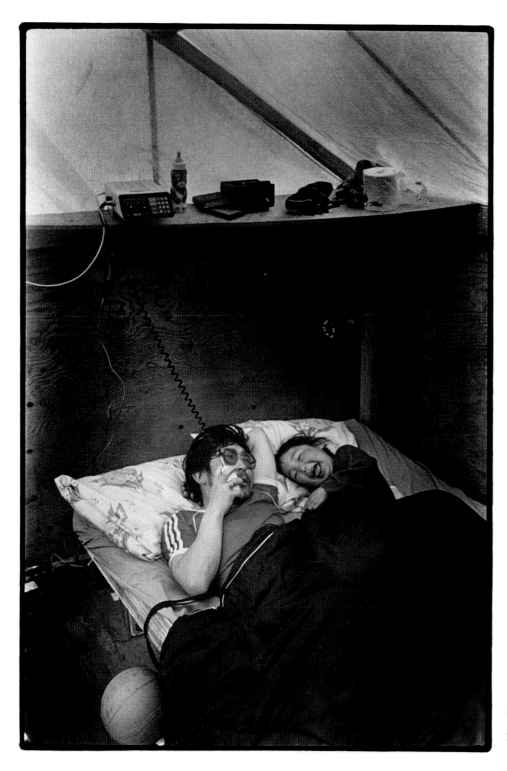

Mike Kaganak and his daughter Alice at Black River
fishcamp, talking by VHF radio to Scammon Bay.

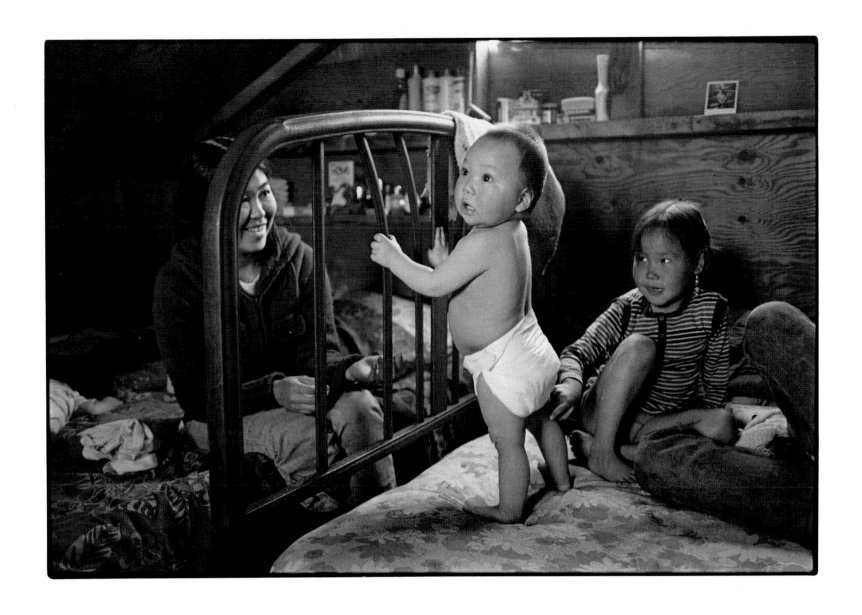

Marie Hoover with her niece and nephew, Samantha and Nicholas, at fishcamp.

Store workers offloading supplies, Sheldon's Point.

Byron Hunter, Elia Charlie, and Oscar Rivers,
Fourth of July at Black River fishcamp.

Commercial fishermen waiting to sell salmon, Bethel.

Arlene and Cynthia Tunutmoak pick edible greens, Black River fishcamp.

The Andrew and Wasuli families berry picking, Kotlik.

Helen, Maggie, and Shirley Wasuli picking salmonberries, Kotlik.

Harvey Alexie, Mountain Village.

THE KUSKOKWIM AND YUKON RIVERS ARE BROAD and shallow by the time they reach the delta region. They meander sluggishly through the tundra plains, carving and recarving their channels and leaving numerous sidewater routes or sloughs. These rivers are a maze to the inexperienced navigator. Side sloughs can save many miles of travel or turn into dead ends. The main river can be deceptively broad. Only the main channel, winding in an invisible, narrow path, is deep enough for safe travel. An experienced boatman knows how to "read" the slight swirls on the surface to find the channel. Once there, the bow of the boat will hunt back and forth from the pressure of these swirls. A traveler missing the channel by just a few yards will sometimes find his boat jammed against a hidden sandbar with the outboard screaming out of the water. It is not uncommon on such occasions for the occupants to be violently thrown from the boat and drowned.

Those who drive the river frequently exchange observations about the changing channels and sandbars as each season requires a renewed assessment of the waterways. During the first few years I lived in Bethel, a long bend upriver could be avoided by turning left off the main river and traveling the mile length of Straight Slough. Arriving again on the main river I could head almost directly across and enter the lower mouth of Church Slough. Over the years a sandbar formed across the mouth of Church Slough and eventually it was shorter to get there via the main river.

There may be no more powerful impulse in the Yup'iks than the desire, when the weather turns warm, to leave the village and set up fishcamp. With the arrival of the first birds there is a sense everywhere that people are anxious to get out of the crowded confines of the village. At breakup everyone keeps a watchful eye, thinking of travel, of setting up camp, of getting on with the summer's activities. Then suddenly the river is free of ice and families begin to move.

The fishcamp survives from earlier, more nomadic times when Yup'ik families moved several times each year in pursuit of foods. Salmon are still the main protein source for villagers who live along the rivers. Camps are established along the Yukon and Kuskokwim and their tributaries where salmon run. To catch, dry, and store enough salmon for the whole year requires serious production. This is not sport fishing by any measure. Long gill nets are employed and hundreds of fish are processed by each family.

Fishcamps along the rivers are small. Usually one to three related families will camp together, though one often finds many separate fishcamps stretched out in a long line along the banks. They may be located as close to the village as a river bend or two, or they may be as far away as thirty miles. Usually the site is in a convenient location for subsistence and commercial fishing and an easy ride back to the village to buy supplies and attend church.

The camp can be as simple as a single whitewall tent, a smokehouse, and a fish rack with the cutting table nearby. More established camps will have substantial cabins, outbuildings, smoke houses, rows of drying racks, steambaths,

Charles Phillip, Kuskokwim river pilot.

and gas-powered Maytag washers. Some camps have small generators to power a CB radio to keep in contact with the village or even to run a television set.

Driving by a fishcamp is a welcome moment of interest on a long boat ride past endless cottonwood trees. A man chops wood or works on an outboard. Over the whole scene wafts the strong but pleasant odor of cottonwood smoke that seeps between the boards of the smokehouse. There is always a friendly wave from someone as they note whether you are a stranger to the area, which direction you appear to be going, and what kind of load you might be carrying. People in rural Alaska keep track of what's going on around them. Everyone waits for news of the salmon's arrival. John Samuelson, well into his eighties, frequently caught the first salmon in the Bethel region. The checker in the grocery store might tell me or KYUK radio might announce on the evening news that John had caught his king.

One day in July, when a few days of unusually sunny weather and wind had reduced Bethel's dirt roads to a dust bowl, Robin announced that she was taking our son Eric across the river to visit the Hoovers, friends from Kasigluk, at their fishcamp for a few days. At four, Eric was old enough to enjoy fishcamp and deserved to go as much as anyone. I dropped them off by boat that afternoon and visited for a while before returning.

The undisputed matriarch of the camp was Anesia Hoover, who we knew would probably be working somewhere directing the operation of cutting, drying, smoking, and storing the enormous quantity of salmon needed for the family. Her two sons, Levi and Tim, had done much of the fishing earlier and were not much in evidence, seeming to appear and quietly take care of heavy work when it was needed. Their wives, Anesia's four adult daughters—Marie, Sylvia, Carrie, and Bertha—and another woman from Kasigluk had fallen into a rhythm of work and relaxation. Nine or more children helped or played about the camp.

From our approach on the river we could see several children playing in the skiffs which the tide had left up on the silt. Spotting us, they disappeared into the brush with

a small dog at their heels, running to the tents to tell the grownups. They were back as we pulled up and helped us carry our gear, the oldest girl leading Eric. A trail led up the bank, past a cabin and several storage sheds to Anesia's tent. Marie was there waiting. A place was found for our little tent by the clearing, next to a storage shed and the basketball hoop. Marie gave us tea in Anesia's tent, which served as the cookhouse. A Pic coil burned in the doorway, keeping out most of the mosquitoes and making an aroma that is familiar to all fishcamps. After tea we walked to the back of the camp where the fish-cutting table stands by a slough that passes the other side of the camp. Sylvia and Anesia were there working in the usual costume, rain pants and aprons made from plastic garbage sacks. They were cutting king salmon into strips or wide double-fillets called "blankets." Next to the cutting table, extensive racks of spruce poles had been constructed. On these the salmon hung, bright red, contrasting with the green foliage of willows.

Anesia and Sylvia used the traditional woman's knife or *uluaq*, a half-circle blade with a handle on top. Several silent cuts were followed by the scratch of the blade being cleaned on the cardboard covering the table. Once the head was cut off, a swift cut laid the belly open. More cuts scalloped across the thick fillets opened the flesh for further air contact. Somehow both fillets opened out neatly into one connected "blanket." The whole thing was held open with a stick from the neat pile at Anesia's feet, and the fish was hung on the rack to dry. Although I have watched women cut fish many times, I am always struck by the efficiency of movement and the meticulous organization of the operation. The women's hands move in a steady rhythm and with uncanny speed and precision. The exact way to cut the fish varies a lot between types of salmon and there are variations between villages. Each woman has learned from her mother or grandmother precisely how to cut fish for the weather conditions and drying methods of her area.

Most fish are preserved by air-drying and smoking. I have seen women spread the thick blood from the backbone bloodline on the surface of the flesh and then shake salt on the flesh from a shaker. They say salt helps keep the flies away. The fish are allowed to dry outdoors for a few days before they are put into the smokehouse. The smokehouse is a porous shack where the fish are hung up on rafters. A smudge fire is made from cottonwood which imparts a fine smoke flavor to the fish. Smoking also protects it from flies and prevents spoiling.

The first salmon to swim up the Kuskokwim River, arriving in Bethel about the first of June, is the king salmon (chinook), weighing from twenty to sixty pounds. On the Kuskokwim most villagers prefer the kings because of their dark red, oil-rich flesh. I have been told that when nets were made of more fragile sinew, kings were not harvested because of the damage they did to them. Concurrent with the kings are the red salmon (sockeye), a smaller lake-spawning fish. These were once abundant but they decreased until 1979, when international treaties limited the Japanese high seas fishery. Since then they have begun to come back.

By the end of June the chum salmon are running, weighing ten to fifteen pounds. They run through most of July and have a lighter colored meat than the kings or reds. Since chums are much smaller and not so rich in oil, they are much easier to dry. They were traditionally thought to have medicinal qualities and are still eaten by many people. Before snowmachines replaced dog teams in the 1960s, the chum salmon was the food harvested for the dogs. Each dog would eat a fish a day. Most people still refer to chums as dog salmon.

In August come the silver salmon (coho), a fine-tasting fish with read meat, about the same size as the chum. Since the silvers arrive so late, when fall weather begins to set in, they were generally not dried like the others. When traders and missionaries arrived bringing salt, the silvers were salted and packed in barrels or they were buried. Now they are often brined in small pieces to make *sulunaq*, which is eaten with seal oil. Or they are simply put in freezers by families who have such luxuries.

Catching a year's supply of fish, thousands of pounds, is a real effort. The salmon are caught with gill nets from 20 to 100 yards long. The net has an opening in the mesh just large enough for the salmon to poke its head through, trapping the fish by its gills. To catch the large kings a net with seven- or eight-inch mesh is used. A six-inch mesh is used on silvers, chums, and reds. White floats hold one edge of the net near the surface and a heavier "leadline" attached to the bottom holds the net vertical in the water. The salmon swim into the net in the murky river water. The big kings sometimes hit the net with great thrashing, and at the very least the added weight of the fish will usually pull one or more floats under water.

Gill nets are employed in two different ways, the set and the drift net. One end of a set net is usually tied to the shore and the other end is tied to a float and anchored out in the river. The net is usually placed in an eddy where the fish linger en route up the river. It is often left there for several weeks and it is checked once or twice a day. This is done by pulling the net over the bow and extracting the fish, a job that in bad weather is more easily said than done. Each family's set net site is respected by others and unless the river changes the same family may use the same site for many years.

Drifting requires a similar net but longer, about 100 yards. The net is deployed from the skiff in a line across the flow of the river. One end is tied to the skiff and the other is tied to a bright orange or red float. The fisherman feeds the net out over the bow as the boat is run at right angles to the current. By rowing or running the outboard at an idle, the net is then held taut, allowing the current to drift the net and boat in a gentle arc down the river. This trick requires some practice. At the end of the drift, which might last as long as an hour, the net is pulled in and the fish are removed. The skiff is then motored upriver for another drift. Experienced fishermen know the exact contours of the river bottom and will work the net back and forth, brushing along the sandbars and eddies where salmon linger.

I've spent many pleasant hours when the weather is good drifting downriver tending a net. Unfortunately on warm clear days the fish tend to swim deeper and the fishing isn't usually as good. Even in good weather, pulling in a loaded net and extracting the fish while standing in a rocking boat is backbreaking work. But it is usually when storms hit and winds and waves start bouncing the boat around that the fish also hit. I've been held up in the middle of the river trying to maintain good footing in a rocking boat as I frantically cleared the net of fish so I could get to shore. Worse yet I've caught one of the river's many sunken snags and fought a terrible snarl of net and fish as the boat hammered up and down. But once in an incoming tide, when the fish tend to run, I caught eighty silver salmon in one hour-long drift—enough fish to last our family for the whole year.

Since the Yup'ik villages are located in a remote part of Alaska, well away from normal job markets, there has been much interest in commercial fishing for income. In 1974, limited-entry permits were issued for the Kuskokwim River to those who had been actively engaged in commercial fishing, mostly local residents. About 830 of them were given out in the next few years. State and federal law mandate that subsistence fishing will take precedence over commercial harvesting. In a given run, the biologists carefully monitor the number of fish in the river. Every family keeps a record of its subsistence catch to turn in for annual data. If the run is strong, the biologists schedule a commercial opening for several hours. This catch is counted and the cycle begins again. There is often controversy about the accuracy of the biologists' numbers, but everyone supports the subsistence priority and the importance of maintaining the species.

Commercial fishing on the Kuskokwim and Yukon rivers requires similar gear to that used for subsistence. Larger skiffs are employed, although any size can be used, and the fish are caught by drift netting. The Department of Fish and Game opens the commercial fishery on the Kuskokwim, usually for six hours at a time. Fishermen will run up or downriver selecting a spot they feel will yield the most fish based on the timing of the tides and the existing weather conditions. The fish are then sold to one of the processors at the dock in Bethel or to one of their tender boats.

According to estimates made by the Alaska Department of Fish and Game, the average fishing income earned by Kusko-kwim permit holders in the eighties was about $6,500 a summer. The lower Yukon fisherman can earn somewhat more because of the greater number of fish and higher prices paid. This moderate income helps pay for boats, snowmachines, rifles, and all those things that allow villagers to carry on with their subsistence living.

One day in late June 1980, after five days of bad weather, Robin and I caught a ride from the village of Scammon Bay to Black River fishcamp. The camp is located about two hours north by boat along the Bering Sea coast toward the mouth of the Yukon, and a number of families who had come to the village for church were heading back. Sebastian Kasayuli took five of us in his newly built wooden boat, driven by a 70-horse outboard. The boat was designed for multipurpose use, but specifically to allow its owner to enter the new commercial herring fishery near Cape Romanzof. We departed at 4 P.M. on an outgoing tide. The weather was the usual overcast, but some holes in the clouds gave brief moments of sun. The route followed the convex curve of the flat tundra beach. The water was very shallow so the boat had to be kept about a quarter of a mile from land to find deep enough water. Some time and distance could be saved by running the boat fast enough to stay up on a plane. After about an hour the first tank of gas, six gallons, ran out and the engine quit. The second tank was hooked up, but the boat could not be run back up on plane because the acceleration lowers the stern, digging the prop into the sand. All Sebastian could do was idle away from the beach for about ten minutes until deep enough water was reached. Then we all moved to the front of the boat, the engine raced, much mud churned up, and we eventually got up on a plane again.

As we approached the mouth of Black River we saw Francis Charlie's boat, loaded with his many children and some friends, about ten women and children in all. They were also returning to the fishcamp from the village. Francis had spotted a beluga whale in the shallow water and was herding the whale to keep it from moving out into deep water. He wasn't carrying a gun, so his only recourse was to wait for Sebastian's arrival so our boat could herd the whale while Francis ran his boat into camp for a gun and harpoon. A third, smaller skiff arrived on the scene. None of the men in it had a gun but they produced a harpoon. In four feet of water the whale couldn't escape the two boats.

About half an hour later Francis returned in his aluminum skiff with one of his daughters driving. He took his position in the bow and directed the boat by waving the rifle. Sebastian saw that the daughter wasn't able to steer well enough, so he motioned Francis to come alongside and he changed places with her. Each time the whale sounded Francis fired a shot. Clearly his rifle was too small, and after many shots the effect on the whale was minimal.

Then a group of boats raced toward us from the mouth of the river. In the bow of one of them sat a man with a much

Harpoon tip.

larger rifle. This boat ran right up the middle of the group and blasted at the whale. I stood up with my camera in one hand and hung onto the gunwale with the other as I tried to take pictures. As more shots were fired, Sebastian zig-zagged to stay with the whale and at one point the others yelled to him to keep out of the line of fire. Harpoons were thrown and a rope snarled in someone's prop. Boats careened around each other as they followed the desperate attempts of the beluga to escape. Then it was over.

The whale, still and floating, was tied between Francis's little boat and our own. As we towed the whale into the mouth of the river, the camp came into view. The gold evening sun shone on tents pitched along the bank, a tiny settlement on the flat, grassy plain. As we passed each tent, people waved and began walking with us until a small procession formed, the children skipping with excitement. For us it was a triumphant entry.

The whale was beached on a slough where a gradually sloping bank would make it easy to pull up for cutting. The children arrived first as the whale was brought to shore and the others came as the rope was passed up the bank. The children swarmed down to examine the whale, identifying its parts, the blowhole, teeth, and bullet holes. They excitedly poked fingers in the bullet and harpoon holes. One found the whale's teats, which were identified by blushing parents. Another found the vagina and the parents turned away.

No butchering was begun until Mike Uttereyuk arrived. With the precision of a surgeon the blubber was first cut away and the pieces thrown up on the bank. The older men began arranging piles of meat for particular families. We were given a hunk of liver for our dinner that evening. Once a proper amount of meat was distributed to the hunters' families, the rest of the whale was dispatched and the pieces distributed among members in the camp. Virtually nothing was left of the whale except for the skull. A couple of days later, Homer Hunter, a carver, pried the teeth out, proposing to use them in some future art work.

The Black River fishcamp is located about a mile inland

from the sea where the tundra is utterly flat and treeless, a plain frequently washed by winds and rain. At first, the view from our tent seemed infinite in all directions. A navigation light placed near the mouth of the river by the Coast Guard to assist ships entering the Yukon channel could be seen a mile or more away. Far to the east the heights of the Kusilvak Mountains were just visible. The river and joining slough were lined with whitewall tents and fish racks where about twenty families lived. A small, single-room store built by the village corporation stood across the river.

The reasons for the location of the camp in this desolate spot are not readily apparent but they are related to currents, wind, and tides. It is on the coast about halfway between the village of Scammon Bay and the mouth of the Yukon. Water from the Yukon enters the Bering Sea and moves south along the coast near the mouth of the Black River and then moves west deeper into the sea. Salmon heading for the Yukon River follow the river water toward the coast, passing in front of the mouth of the Black River. Tides pulse the Yukon's fish-laden water into the Black River, making it an ideal location for fishing. Ideal, that is, when the winds and currents direct the Yukon waters into the Black.

Sometimes winds blow the other direction. In 1980 and for the previous two years, the winds had prevailed from the east, blowing the Yukon waters out away from Black River. The camp was scraping for fish. Usually they had a choice of kings or chums. But now in their desperation, they were even drying humpies, a much smaller salmon, to fill up their racks. When a commercial period was called, the fishermen drove their boats north into the mouth of the Yukon and did well. We heard that in later years when the winds came from the northwest, the fishcamp did a killing job of commercial fishing, better than anyone else on the Yukon.

I walked along the river with Francis Charlie to his set net. He eyed it, exposed on the mud by the tide. He leaned back against the bank for a while with his shotgun handy and I took a picture. He'd noted that herring gulls had been eating some of the fish caught in his net so he wanted to shoot a gull and place it on a stick to ward off other gulls.

He also seemed just to enjoy the excuse for sitting quietly looking out across the almost empty landscape. The uniform gray of the water and sky was separated only by a narrow band of tundra across the river. Looking toward the sea even that minimal line disappeared into the grayness. Looking around he said, "I really like it here."

No one lives permanently now on the Black River. They used to. There was enough population some sixty years ago that a man named Frank Kern built a trading post up the river, just below the spot where the river widens into a shallow lake. Later the store was owned by Northern Commercial Co. At the suggestion of his son, Jack, Harry Wilson took us by boat about twenty miles up the Black River to the two run-down store buildings that stand at the highest point for many miles. As soon as we arrived we climbed out of the boat and headed toward the buildings, but Jack called us back to his father. Harry waited for our complete attention before he began.

He told us the story of two families who once lived down toward the coast. A combination of southwest winds and high tides flooded this flat land. One of the families arose in the middle of the night, finding their house severely flooded. They raced to their boat and only later thought of their friends. They were all found drowned in their home. His story concluded with the thought that people should pay attention to the needs of others as much as their own.

Harry said that families then moved inland, up the river to the spot where the old trading post was located. It was then known, translated from Yup'ik, as the "wintering-in place." Harry thought that Northern Commercial Co. operated the store into the 1950s. By then most people had relocated either up to the Yukon River or down to the village of Scammon Bay with its school and church. The Black River remains a favored area for hunting and fishing. What really startled us as we stood by the old stores and examined the nearby grave sites was the sheer noise of the birds. There was a continuous loud roar of honking and cackling from ducks, geese, cranes, swans.

When he had heard at Scammon Bay that Robin and

"Chuki" (Lucy) George, Umkumiut fishcamp.

I were going to the fishcamp, Carlie Akerelrea had told us with affection that we would "see lots of dirty kids at Black River." Dirty and happy kids, he might have said. The camp, like most fishcamps, is a wonderful place for children during the summer. There is a strict rule that all kids must stay away from the river. The rest is wide open space for an infinite variety of activities.

While we were at fishcamp, the weather remained overcast with frequent rain. On the morning of the Fourth of July we lay in our warm sleeping bags inside our small, rain-splattered mountaineering tent until 11 A.M. waiting for the sounds of camp life to begin. Homer Hunter drove by with a boatload of kids and yelled to us that a Fourth of July cele-bration was going to occur near Billy Rivers' and Francis Charlie's camps. I yelled back to ask what time and immedi-ately realized it was a foolish question. In village life when you are told that something will happen it happens right then. Because the weather had been disagreeable it had been decided that morning to hold a celebration for the benefit of tent-bound kids.

The races began with about ten families participating. The first was the little kids' race. Mothers holding toddlers waited at the line. At the word "go" the kids were launched in the correct direction and they staggered and teetered, arms flailing, seemingly driven onward by the push of the mothers' yells. One little girl, "Mousy" Charlie, burst into tears, disconcerted by the blast of cheering. Wailing, she stopped walking altogether. Boxes of goods had been do-nated for prizes. They were from the corporation store, John Amukon's store, and from Francis Charlie's store, a wall tent behind us. The little ones got candy. There were rolls of paper towels, soaps, Crackerjacks, handcream, toilet paper, Crisco, Worcestershire sauce, and cigarettes for the adults. These gifts were liberally handed out to all the participants.

Then followed races for older kids, a fifty-yard run to a clothesline and back. Then a tug-of-war with kids choosing sides, straining, and the sudden release with kids falling laughing into the muddy tundra. Then the women, teeth gritted and determined, had their tug-of-war while the men and children cheered. Robin and I both ran races. "Sometimes we have a fish-cutting contest," Homer told us. "But this year we have too few fish—not enough to play around with." We heard too of a diaper-hanging race, where two women would hold a clothesline and shake it while two men would compete to hang the most diapers.

There were prizes left over and more races run. After it was all over people drove their boats back to their camps, loaded with happy kids and armloads of prizes. As the rains started up again Robin and I agreed that this had been one of the best Fourth of July celebrations we'd ever experienced.

Later that afternoon Tony Ulak told us he had enough room in his boat to give us a ride back to Scammon Bay. We packed everything up except the tent, holding out that one dry place until we were certain of departure. We were invited into the next tent to have coffee, a stay that turned into dinner as we waited for Tony to clear his nets. During the day the wind had shifted from the south to the east, a good wind for southern travel. When it was time to go we donned all our rain gear and lashed all luggage tight. In the twenty-foot open skiff it would obviously be a wet trip. Tony said he had promised his wife that he'd turn back if the waves got too rough. We left at 8:30 P.M. Blaise Tinker had departed about twenty minutes before. Reaching the Bering Sea we found that low clouds made the visibility poor. Tony kept about 300 yards out from the thin shoreline, staying just close enough to see it yet far enough out to stay in deep water. We all strained our eyes to keep in contact with that thin line of land. After forty-five minutes we spotted Blaise ahead. He'd gotten into the shallows and was idling out to deeper water. Tony couldn't slow down to help as we too would be mired down. He could only wave from a safe distance and pass by.

The curve of the coast directed us more to the east and the boat was pounded more and more by waves. Fog and rain closed in and sometimes we couldn't see the shoreline. Tony tied a rope to the gunwale and held it tight in his gloved right hand as he stood at the tiller. "This will help me from being thrown out," he said. I kept squinting to the south hoping to see the mountains of Cape Romanzof, but the weather had closed in too much. I wondered if the wind would shift. If we lost sight of land a shifting wind would lead us in the wrong direction. Tony asked us if we could see the shore. Having assumed that he could see better than we could, we were unsettled. We answered that we could, "just barely, at times, yes." "Good," he said, and explained that he'd broken his glasses and couldn't see very well without them. We continued our watch with much added effort. Finally I could see a snowfield, ghost-like in the gray twilight fog. "That's our mountain," said Tony. He smiled with relief. A little further on, with the fog dense around us, he observed, "We're in the river now." Puzzled, we asked how he could tell. He replied, "I can smell the bushes," and so we could. Soon we were tying the boat to the landing. With heavy packs and wet rain gear we trudged happily the quarter mile from the boat into the village.

As the summer progresses everyone keeps a careful eye on the evolving weather. Drying fish must be protected from the effects of dampness; women watch for the perfect combination of sun and rain for the ripening berries and check the length of the grass as a sign of the severity of the coming winter. Berry picking comes in late July and continues into August. There are four kinds of berries and they ripen in a predictable order as the season shifts toward fall: salmonberries, blueberries, crowberries, and then cranberries. Over the summer women watch the weather and speculate about the coming harvest. The berries' abundance, sweetness, and water content will depend on sun, rain, and temperatures. When they are ready, boats loaded with families drive many miles, traveling narrow streams back into the tundra to favorite picking grounds.

In late July 1983 I went berry picking with Maggie and Al Wasuli's family in Kotlik. Our boat held Maggie and Al, their three girls, Maggie's mother, Regina Andrews, and myself. A second boat carried other family and friends. We set off to a favorite picking spot about two hours by boat to the lakes at the headwaters of the Kotlik River. The river became narrower and narrower, but Al knew the way so well

Alice Rivers with her son Oscar, guarding her salmon net from seagulls, Black River fishcamp.

that we could drive the boat at high speed through the curves. We came to a lake at the farthest navigable point and stopped.

Everyone took a bucket and spread across the tundra to pick salmonberries. These orange-red berries look very much like small clumps of salmon eggs, hence their English name. They are particularly high in vitamin C. The blueberries and cranberries that ripen later are more dense, and a picker can kneel or squat in one place for a while. As Regina said, "The salmonberries are the hardest to pick because you have to move constantly on your feet." Helen, Al and Maggie's three-year-old, was given a cup, but she ate everything she picked. Someone was always yelling to her not to eat all the berries, fearing she'd get sick. Maggie later had her drink seal oil, hoping to counteract the effect of the berries.

Yup'iks are determined berry pickers. I've seen boats return loaded with three or four wood barrels full of berries. The favorite traditional use of berries is *akutaq*. It is made by mixing a light froth of beaten seal oil or reindeer tallow with snow and adding half-frozen berries. In some parts of the delta pressed whitefish or pike and sometimes greens are included. Nowadays Crisco, with a little sugar, is often used, making a base that resembles bakery icing in texture and flavor. It is usually kept in a cold corner of the house or storm porch and served cold. The half-frozen berries in the sweet, cold mixture make a delicious dessert which has earned the English name "Eskimo ice cream."

In 1975, Maggie Lind, an elder from Bethel, testified at a Bureau of Land Management hearing. "In the summertime we get lots of berries; salmonberries, black [crow] berries, and we put them in the baskets and put them in the water and in the fall we put them up for food, you know. Make *akutaq* which is our main food, and if we don't eat *akutaq* and we're out in the cold traveling, we get cold. We have to have something to keep our feet, our blood warm" (Nunam Kitlusisti 1976:10).

Ponds Freeze, Worst of the Moon

Nanvat Cikutiit, Iralull'er

Bethel.

Maggie Wasuli taking children to school during freezeup, Kotlik.

Paul Gregory with a blackfish fish trap, Bethel.

Alan Hanson and Joseph Smith
resetting a blackfish trap, Alakanuk.

Bringing in firewood, Bethel.

Pilot Station.

PONDS FREEZE, WORST OF THE MOON

Storm in Bethel.

Elvina Turner, a nurse, visiting Lucy Link, Bethel.

PONDS FREEZE, WORST OF THE MOON

Watching dancing at the Tundra Fest, Chevak.

Kwethluk Health Aide Betty Guy with Molly Owens of Akiak, at Kwethluk.

Pete Abruska and Sinka Sakar at winter trapping camp.

Checking beaver snares under the ice
with the snowmachine headlight.

Father Guest blesses the waters for a prosperous fishing season in the coming year, Napaskiak.

AFTER FAMILIES RETURN FROM BERRY CAMP, the local stores fill up with people restocking for moose hunting. Villagers on the coast supplement their fish diet with sea mammals—seal, walrus, and sometimes beluga whale. Inland people hunt moose and caribou. Caribou roam in small herds in the mountains to the south of the delta region and are generally hunted by snowmachine. Moose range the forested inland regions.

During the fall the Department of Fish and Game allows a moose hunt. With the increasing speed and power of boats, many hunters now travel 200 to 300 miles inland up the Kuskokwim or Yukon rivers to good hunting grounds. Some of the upriver villagers, people who are traditionally rival Eskimo groups or are Athabaskan Indians, feel the hunting pressure from the downriver people as well as from sport hunters who fly in from the Anchorage area. The pressure on the moose population makes it more difficult for families to get the meat they need during the prescribed time period. Sometimes the game is harvested illegally, as legal seasons do not always coincide with local needs.

Pete Bobby of Lime Village, a Tanaina Athabaskan village at the eastern edge of the region, attended a hearing in Bethel to talk about this conflict: "We had no more food in Lime Village, so I caught a moose. Even though we had many kids to feed, we shared the moose meat with other people who also needed food. Someone turned me in for killing a moose out of season. The State knew that it is impossible to get store goods into Lime Village in winter, but they took the moose meat away and fined me $50. I think it is odd that I hunt by foot with moccasins on and am tried for hunting for my family when they are hungry, and airplanes land all the time right in front of my village, shoot moose and caribou, cut off the heads, and take off, leaving the meat behind. State of Alaska says that you cannot give meat away to your friend, yet that is our way of life" (Nunam Kitlusisti 1977:3).

Currently the laws allow for hunting game out of season if the accused can prove that the family had no other recourse. Our Bethel judge, Chris Cooke, once heard the case of an elderly man accused of killing a beaver out of season. This judge was known for being sympathetic in such cases. As he remembers it, he made sure the man understood the charges and knew that he had a right to be represented before he accepted a guilty plea. He then asked for an explanation of the circumstances before deciding on a sentence.

"I asked him if he had anything to say on his own behalf before sentence was imposed since there is a defense of necessity [need for food]. At that point he said he'd been out camping and hunting on the Tuluksak River for a number of days and that he'd broken his false teeth and couldn't eat, couldn't chew his food. He wanted to use the beaver's teeth to replace his false ones and that the beaver teeth were very good for that. At that point my judicial demeanor left me and I called a recess." The sentence was minimal.

By the middle of October the temperatures rapidly decline and the wind has a decided bite. The cold is felt more at this time of year because we've adapted to the warmth of summer. Men return from moose hunting and families work long hours at putting up the meat. Short trips for last-minute bird hunting are made, but sometimes boats must be chopped out of the ice in the mornings. Facing the harsh fall winds and cold spray from the choppy waters makes traveling by open boat very uncomfortable. Villagers make final trips into Bethel to buy fuel and food, to stock up for the period of freezeup.

Depending on the weather, the rivers can freeze in a matter of days or freezeup can be a slow process, taking almost a month before the ice is solid enough for snowmachines. Travel all but ceases and, as the period of confinement goes on, people become more and more anxious for winter activities to begin.

After living in the region for a few years I came to understand why some people actually prefer the winter. During the summer months all surface travel is confined to the rivers and lakes. At freezeup these river systems become thoroughfares once more and winter trails open up. The tundra, which has been closed to travel all summer, will soon be accessible on foot or by snowmachine in any direction.

Fall is a dangerous time because the ice on rivers, lakes, and sloughs freezes inconsistently. One side of the river may be solid for travel whereas the other side may not. In addition, an early snow can insulate a thin layer of ice which will slow down the development of solid ice. Often one or two people misjudge the fall ice and go through. Some don't survive. An inexperienced traveler avoids going anywhere others have not first gone. As Henry Ivanoff, an Alaska Native from north of the region, laughingly said, "I don't go out on the river with my snowmachine until I see Eddie Hoffman drive his oil truck out there." Young people in the villages wait for the elders to begin their activities on the ice.

Halloween comes as a pleasant diversion during the restricted mobility of freezeup. In old times there was a fall festival, *qaariitaarvik*, in which children wearing masks and carrying bowls were led from house to house to be given gifts of food. Josephine Tom remembered that "around the time that Halloween started, we put our masks on and went into houses five times" (Kalikaq Yugnek 1977:124). Nowadays villagers refer to Halloween as a sort of time marker in the fall just as we might refer to Memorial Day. Children can be seen dashing from house to house in the icy wind or blowing snow wearing costumes from Ninja Turtles to Frankenstein. One opens the door to a row of masked faces, Donald Duck, Superman, and Dracula, all surrounded by beautiful fur ruffs.

Usually by the middle of November the ice is solid enough for safe travel. As soon as the river is safe for walking, people begin jigging for fish. A hole is punched through the ice with a chipper. A hook and line are tied to a short stick and moved up and down by hand to catch whitefish and, later, pike.

One day our Yup'ik neighbors, Bill and Bessie Atseriak, invited my wife to go jigging. Robin dressed warmly in her skin boots, a colorful Eskimo-style parka with white fox ruff, and fur mitts. Bessie and Bill arrived in their National Guard snowmachine suits. The three drove down to the river and settled themselves on the ice, Robin at a hole a little away from the other two. My wife was lucky and she teased her friends about the small pile of fish she soon had at her feet. A snowmachine appeared in the distance carrying two unfamiliar white people. As Robin squatted at the hole, her head down, the machine rumbled to a stop close by and two pairs of boots stepped up. In carefully enunciated English a voice asked, "May . . . I . . . take . . . your . . . picture?" "Sure," she answered, turning her blue eyes up at them. The men backed away and took off on their machine, leaving Bessie and Bill in stitches.

Right after freezeup, when the ice is still thin, is the time when nets are put in the river for the winter. To do this, a series of holes is chopped in the ice and, using a stick, a line is fed underwater from hole to hole until it extends under the ice for several yards. Then the net is attached to the line and pulled into the water where it hangs vertically under the ice between the first and last holes. The net is checked for fish by tying a rope at the far end and pulling it up through the opposite hole to remove the fish. It is then reset to be checked in another day or two. Poles mark the placement of the net for the months until the owner decides to pull it later in the winter. Checking the net regularly can be bitter work but the reward is fresh fish, a welcome change from dried salmon.

Yup'iks, like any of us, enjoy variety in their diet. The smallest freshwater fish that is harvested is the blackfish. It is six to eight inches long and lives in small streams. It's an extremely hardy fish and is a favorite pet. When there are children in the house I have frequently been offered tea at the table next to a lone blackfish in a jar of water. Blackfish are caught with traps. Traditionally made of wood, these traps now are more frequently made of wire mesh. The traps are conical in form with an inner funnel at one end through which the fish enter. They are often put in place in the fall before freezeup, but I've seen them set almost any time during the winter. Johnny Hawk of Eek told me once that he saw places where the blackfish were so numerous that they melted the ice in the middle of the winter. The blackfish is sometimes used as insurance. A trap can be left for weeks at a time as the fish keep alive on the nutrients in the stream. If other foods run out, or someone wants some fresh fish, the trap is pulled out, the fish are extracted, and the trap is reset.

In the latter 1970s and into the 1980s the villagers, particularly those near the coast, were bothered about the growing numbers of beavers that were disturbing the blackfish streams by building dams. Beavers are lot of trouble to trap, and pelt prices were very low at that time, so the beavers were free to do their worst.

One March I accompanied a young man, Nick Alexie, to Old Camp north of Bethel near the Johnson River, to check his blackfish traps. Nick was recognized by the Alaska State Council on the Arts for his skill at building wood traps and I was asked to photograph him. We traveled about two hours north of Bethel by snowmachine, passing Joe Chief who was checking his beaver snares in a snow-covered stream. In the middle of the open tundra, Old Camp was distinguished by willows edging a small stream. I noted a couple of snug sod houses used by hunters. Nick said his father wanted him to check the traps even though they'd just been put in the day before. Nick said that blackfish ran strongest this time of year. One of the ways of placing a trap is to dig a hole through the ice into the stream; the trap is then supported vertically below the hole with the rim two to three inches below the surface of the water. The blackfish come up to the hole to get air and then swim down, entering the trap. In one spot Nick dug a hole to place one of his traps and found dead blackfish. He noted that this was a good sign because they were desperate for air and many would be caught. From the trap he emptied about forty pounds of wriggling fish into a gunnysack lined with a garbage bag.

"I'd been up to the dance festival at St. Mary's," Alma Keyes of Kotlik once told me. "When I returned home I wanted to eat some blackfish. That same day I returned I made a blackfish trap out of a piece of wire mesh laying around. My sister and I took it out to a nearby stream and put it in. I wanted to taste blackfish right away so we waited right there a little while for the trap to catch enough. We got lots of 'em."

Thanksgiving comes and is celebrated with moose or rabbit, turkey or herring, but the feast favorite, akutaq, is always served. The days grow very short as the sun skims in a long arc hugging the horizon. The snow glows violet and pink for hours of sunrise followed a short time later by a long, lingering sunset. Figures on the street are recognized by familiar parkas as faces disappear into fur ruffs to be protected from the ever present wind.

On a day when the temperatures rise to zero or the wind abates, people gravitate to the outdoors to split wood, check rabbit snares, jig for fresh fish, or go "chase foxes." Riverbanks are crowded with children who speed down onto the ice in improvised sleds made from sheets of cardboard or inverted outboard covers. Visiting increases with the cold weather and the holidays. School tournaments, village league basketball, Christmas, followed by Russian Christmas for some, meetings, and dance festivals fill the winter months and provide opportunities for travel and visits with relatives.

In February of 1982, I was invited to photograph fur trapping with Sinka Sakar and Pete Abruska, who at that time both lived in Chauthbaluk. It was a special occasion. Sinka, fifty-three, had recovered from a stroke. Pete, seventy-seven, was nearing the end of his outdoor career. It seemed as if these two men wanted to have this one last trapping experience together. I packed up my snowmachine sled and departed from Bethel for the 150-mile trip up the Kuskokwim River to Aniak. There had been a thaw in the middle of the winter and without any additional snow the river was covered with glassy smooth ice. Within five miles of home, I had twice lost control of the sled on the slick ice and the third time I spun around, smashing it so badly it could no longer be used. A plastic camera bag was cracked but the equipment was OK. I returned home and flew up to Aniak. I borrowed a machine and sled there and went across the river to stay with our longtime friends Jackie Feigon and "Gib" Gibson until the trip started.

The temperature had settled into a constant 25 below zero, with winds from the north making travel on the river very cold. Every night Gib talked by CB radio with Sinka, ten miles upriver, to discuss the weather. The trip was delayed day after day, as we waited for the cold snap to break. Sinka was protective of Pete's age but finally on Saturday night, with no let-up in sight, Sinka told me to come on up the next day for a noon departure. The following morning I left Aniak. I pulled out on the smooth river ice, the 340 Yamaha easily pulling the heavy sled. But after only a few hundred yards, the machine slowed. I stopped, tipped it on its side, and found the plastic slide rail suspension system to be quite warm. The slight trace of snow wasn't enough to provide the necessary cooling for the slide rail even traveling at slow speeds. For a couple of miles I had to drive along the river-banks, steering over patches of blown snow to cool the rails until I could turn off on an overland trail the rest of the way.

At Sinka's home I found that his two teenage sons, Sinka, Jr., and Nick, would accompany us, making five on the trip. Pete was still loading his sled. He first loaded the stove, which was made from the bottom of a fifty-gallon trash barrel. He said, "You're going to love this stove," as if anyone wouldn't love any stove in these temperatures. He packed the whitewall tent, stovepipe, bags holding an assortment of traps and snares, and cans of fuel. With three machines pulling three heavy sleds, we proceeded slowly up the smooth river ice, hugging the edge where the trace of snow allowed some control. After about three hours we stopped at the almost abandoned village site of Napaimute and warmed ourselves over a pot of fresh coffee at George Hoffman's cabin.

Continuing on, we crossed long stretches of glassy ice. Great care had to be exercised to keep the wind from blowing the machines and sleds sideways because the slightest edge of ice will catch a runner and snap it off. We stopped for the night at Mary and Marius ("Morrie") Hofseth's house a couple of miles above Napaimute. They had painted the place entirely white inside so that the one hanging Coleman lantern made the room unusually bright in the long winter night.

Morrie told us how he lost his arm. During the winter of 1974 he was traveling downriver by himself on a snow-machine. The track became caked with ice. Attempting to clear it, he reached into the track and accidentally hit the throttle. His arm was caught. He couldn't reach his tools to release the tension on the track so he sat there for some time trying to work his arm loose. Knowing he would die without help, he lay there long enough for his arm to freeze, cut it off, and walked the couple of miles downriver to a nearby cabin for help.

The next day, still fighting the glare ice, we continued on up the river against the strong north winds with the temperature near minus 20° F. After twenty miles Sinka led us into the mouth of the Oskawalik River. Pete explained that the river's name comes from the word for dog harness, which was perhaps inspired by its many branches. After four miles we came to a place protected by trees where the two men judged there was an adequate supply of dry wood. The 8-by-10-foot wall tent was put up and the stove was assembled. Noting that the stovepipe Pete brought lacked a damper, I found a tin can left from a previous camp and fashioned one to slip into it. With the fire roaring and a rush of draft air, Pete said, "Now the stove talks." A hole was dug through the ice for water and small dead trees were felled for firewood. Our work done for the day, we sat on rounds of wood, huddled around the stove in the warm tent, and we ventured outside only when necessary. The slightest decline in the fire would rapidly cool the tent. As Sinka put it, we "bullshitted" our way through the evening. We all used two sleeping bags to ward off the cold. Thankfully, one of the boys was quick to arise each morning and set a new fire to warm the tent for a civilized awakening.

The purpose of the trip was to set snares for beaver and marten. There has been a growing population of beaver in the delta but unfortunately the prices have been declining. One fur buyer suggested that the only way to profit from trapping beaver was to send the pelts to be tanned and then have the women make beaver hats, which go for good prices.

For the next few days we traveled along the river, stopping at beaver lodges and setting snares. The position of each lodge was carefully studied. Holes were chipped down through three or four feet of ice to the water. Sinka and Pete poked sticks down through the holes and probed the contours of the stream bottom trying to locate the beaver runs from the house to their food source. Often, a second or third hole had to be chipped before the snare could be effectively positioned. Eventually Pete, tired of the chipping, asked Sinka if he'd mind his using the chain saw to cut holes. Sinka didn't. The holes were rapidly but noisily cut and the snares were more quickly set. Meanwhile Sinka's sons set snares nearby in the woods for marten.

On the second day Sinka's son Junior caught a marten in one of the traps. As he brought it back to the sled Sinka quickly moved to his side, whispering that he should give it to Pete. His son held it out to Pete, who said in a generous tone, "Oh, thank you, how lucky I am. Oh, this is wonderful." Sinka later told me that it was customary to give the first catch to the elders. The next day, when Nick caught a beaver in a trap, it was also presented to Pete and again Pete thanked him profusely.

As the sun lowered each afternoon, everyone continued working until it was almost dark. When it got too dark a snowmachine would be pulled up to check a previously drilled hole. With the hood unlatched and tipped up the headlight could be beamed down into the hole. Then the whole bottom of the river was well illuminated and the beaver routes easily recognized.

By that time of the evening we were all getting quite cold. We raced back down the river to the camp, hurriedly did the chores as quickly as possible, and hovered around the warm stove for the rest of the evening. I remarked how clean winter camping is, since it is too cold for bacteria to form on dirty dishes. Pete responded by saying that his grandfather, a Russian who lived well into his nineties, told him, "Never be afraid of anything, no man, no woman, nothing." He said this with firm conviction. Later he shifted into a less serious mood saying, "The real boss is the poop. When that poop wants to come, nothing can stop him. That's right, the poop is the real boss. No man, no game warden, no governor, no president, no Pope—no nothing can stop the poop

when it wants to come. The poop is the real boss."

An old man, Pete moved slowly. He chipped ice carefully, directing each blow to gain the greatest effect. Down on his knees setting a snare, he'd deftly snag anything he needed with the ice chipper and pull it near so he wouldn't have to get up. He had difficulty pulling the starter rope on his chain saw, but he'd work at it. Often one of the boys was nearby to help him. Pete said simply, "I do the best I can." One morning one of the sons offered a small bowl of warm water for washing. With great glee Pete said, "Oh, thank you very much." After washing he said, "That was wonderful," as if he'd just finished a hot shower. Once as we sat through the evening Pete noted that the wool felt packs in his boots were worn thin. He selected a piece of cardboard from a box and carefully cut out insoles to add warmth to his boots.

After four days, Sinka hinted that if the weather didn't warm up he knew that Pete would worry about whether he had cut enough wood for his family. He suggested we leave the following day. It was Pete and Sinka's plan to come and go all through the next couple of months.

A few months later Sinka told me that their total catch had been fourteen to sixteen beaver (about $40 a pelt), fourteen marten ($60 to $80 each), and two otter ($250 each) for one and a half to two months of trapping. I estimated that this gave them a possible total of $2,260 for both their efforts, not counting the expense of gas and equipment. Their spring trapping had supplied them with some necessary income, but I felt that both men were doing it mainly to enjoy the skills they'd learned to use so well and the pleasure of the adventure together. And it turned out that this season of trapping was Pete's last before he died.

One winter morning an excited Kriska Evans, a man from up the river whose family background is both Eskimo and Athabaskan, called me on the phone. He said he had a story to tell me that he'd just written about his childhood. It was about moose hunting with his father, which they used to do with dogs in the spring. Today, dogs are prohibited and the seasons are in the fall and later in the winter in order to avoid taking cows carrying calves. Kriska waited for me to get the tape recorder turned on and began.

"I used to live up in Red Devil [a mercury mining town about 230 miles upriver from Bethel]. When we hunted moose we did it in April when the snow crust was strong enough to support the weight of a man, but not a moose. That way a man would have an advantage.

"One day, when I was just twelve years old, my father took me out hunting about fifty miles away up in the George River area. We were traveling by dog team going along. Suddenly the dogs smelled something and picked up the pace. My father, who was riding in the sled, said, 'See, the dogs smell something.' He was smiling like a little boy watching the dogs speed down the trail. Suddenly we hit a root and the sled jammed to a halt. My dad was thrown forward. As I reached down to grab him I saw a moose up ahead dodge behind some trees, just a glimpse. I said, 'Dad, I saw a moose up there.' He said, 'You couldn't have. The tracks show that it would be at least five miles away.'

"'No, Dad, I seen it, I seen it!' I went forward to the dogs, unhooked all six of them, and they took off running down the trail. We ran after them for a quarter of a mile, then stopped and listened. . . . Silence. Dad said, 'We don't hear any barking. You didn't see a moose.'

"'I seen it, Dad, I seen it.'

"We ran another quarter of a mile and stopped . . . Silence. Dad said, 'Why don't we hear something if there is a moose nearby?' Again I said, 'I seen it, I seen it, I seen it up the trail.' We ran another quarter mile . . . Silence. Now my dad was getting angry, saying, 'You let those dogs loose too quickly. That moose will get plenty angry and the dogs might be injured.' We ran just a little further and then we heard some barking over in the opening. When we got to where we could see, there was the moose in the middle of the opening ringed by our six dogs. Dad was really happy, like a child. When I picked up my gun Dad said, 'No, don't shoot. Those are our hunting dogs. Let them have the moose for a while.'

"Our leader, Red, stood about twenty feet in front of that moose. He looked right at the face of that moose. Then he ran fast ten feet at the moose and jumped up and landed between the horns right on the head and neck and held on. The moose shook its head and threw the dog off about ten to twenty feet. Old Red stood again in front of that moose. Again he dashed toward it and jumped again onto its neck. Again the moose threw him off. My dad just sat there watching all this with a big smile. Finally he said, 'Now's the time. Shoot him four inches below his hump. Don't shoot him in the head because that will make him really mad—he'll see red and be dangerous to our dogs.' This paralyzes the moose without enraging it. So I took up the gun, it was just a 22. I shot, pang! 'Shoot again,' he said. Pang, and pang again. Slowly the moose slowed down. 'Look, he's going to fall.' The dogs jumped in nipping at its legs as the moose slowly fell into the snow. Our dogs just stood there wagging their tails."

Time of Going Around, Time of Drumming

Uivik, Cauyarvik

Wearing a mask he made, John McIntyre (left) from Eek dances with Joe Chief, Jr., from Bethel.
Joe's mask was made by Alexie Issac, also from Bethel.

St. Mary's men receiving potlatch gifts of *akutaq* and frozen salmon, Pilot Station.

Natalia Kelly, Anna Nick, and Agnes Polty of Pilot Station examine potlatch gifts, St. Mary's.

Jimmy Paukan of St. Mary's and Raphael Jimmie and Gregory Joe, Sr.,
of Mountain Village, drumming at the Pilot Station potlatch.

Edward Aguchak with Scammon Bay dancers.

Magdalene Hoelscher of Hooper Bay joins Joe Ayagarak, Jr., and the Chevak dancers, Mountain Village.

Martina John, Paul Agimuk, and Francis Usugan, Toksook Bay dancers, at the St. Mary's dance festival.

Kirt Bell from Hooper Bay sings "Goodnight, Ladies," as he leaves an evening of dancing.

Mary Ann Sundown (left) of Scammon Bay dances with Helen H. Smith, Katherine Bell, and Magdalene Hoelscher, all of Hooper Bay, at *Cama-i* (greetings) Dance Festival, Bethel.

ONE LATE AFTERNOON AT PILOT STATION, a young woman looked out the window in the gathering dusk toward the Yukon River. "Look out across the river! See all the lights of the snowmachines coming! That's what really makes us excited!"

There are a number of traditional celebrations of sharing within a village and between villages that go back for many generations. One important event is still held today at Pilot Station on the Yukon. I was told the celebration was called *curukaq*, meaning to rush the hosting village, a celebration roughly analogous to the traditional "Messenger Feast" or *kevgiq* (Morrow 1984:131). In English, villagers simply call it a potlatch, a rather generic title used for a variety of events. The *curukaq* is the largest group ritual that remains from the old days.

It is among other things a competition between villages. Plans are made far in advance with supposedly great secrecy. Just a few days before the event, a delegation is sent over from the host village to a neighboring village to make the formal invitation, each village hoping to be the first to do the inviting. I was told that one year the neighboring villages sent delegations and the two parties met at the halfway point on the trail. The host village invites their guests to visit for a few days and nights of singing and dancing and they give gifts to everyone from the visiting village. A few weeks or a month later the guest village reciprocates.

I have been invited to attend many potlatches and dances over the years to make photographs and tape interviews. The difficulty of photographing in small, dark community halls was offset by the fact that both dancers and audience fluidly exchange places throughout the event while small children walk directly through the performance space, unmindful of the dancers. I could move about freely. The taped interviews came naturally as well since they were a sort of extension of the abundant visiting that takes place at these events. All of the quotations below come from these tapes.

David Friday is an active dancer and drummer in his thirties. He lives in Chevak. He explained, "There used to be a feeling of togetherness then, the whole community was there. During the spring, summer, and fall the people are all over. But at that time, at the festival, it was the community get-together. A lot of people come together in that one setting. You'd be hearing stories, their songs that they made, the older people, even some older ladies used to make their own songs."

In fact, the *kevgiq* was sometimes held in the summer, but the festivals have generally evolved to the winter season over the years. The details of different celebrations varied from area to area in the region and so, with greater mobility of families and intermarriage, accompanied by past pressures from the missionaries, the festivals have been subject to redefinition and refinement of traditional elements.

Preparation for a potlatch can begin months in advance as villagers begin to make and buy gifts. In the old days food and skin clothing were given. Generosity brought prestige and this still is true today. The receiving village works hard to prepare gifts that are similar in worth to the ones they have received and to invite their hosts within a month or so. As David Friday continued, "They bring part of their catch for give-away. I used to see some seal skins, whole skins, tomcods, poked fish, Eskimo foods they been saving for that. They take pride in bringing those foods there." Sometimes villagers would present such lavish gifts as skin coats to their guests. Years later these gifts are remembered with admiration.

A substantial portion of the gifts are given by a host family or families at each potlatch. The sponsoring family does this to present a child to the assembled communities. If a boy is presented it is generally to proclaim that he has become a hunter, perhaps by shooting his first bird or a small animal. A girl is presented when she has picked berries for the first time or has begun to take on a woman's role in some other way. When the potlatch begins, the child stands on a seal skin before the assembled people to be presented by the father or the grandparent who is hosting the event.

This short introductory speech honors the child's namesake. Children are often named after a relative who dies around the time of their birth and through the child, the ancestor is present at the potlatch. This was true to an even greater extent at the traditional "Feast to the Dead," *elriq*, in which the dead were provided for with gifts to the namesake. Noel Polty, a Pilot Station elder, told me that "we will never give up these potlatches because they remind us of those that have passed away."

There remains a strong feeling that the deceased are in attendance at a potlatch. Chuna McIntyre, in his thirties, is an artist and dancer from Eek who has devoted much of his life to studying and performing traditional dance. He explained the feeling to me this way, "As you know we believe in reincarnation, that movement in families can transcend [death]. When someone does something that Grandpa used to do, that to us is a great moment of discovery, that Grandpop is still here. You know, we are so strong in connection with each other that we look for movements that we recognize from each other."

The movements of favorite dancers are remembered long after them in their dances. "Movements we feel can transcend time and space within families," Chuna says, "because we believe in this cycle, this whole cycle of life." One of his favorite songs expresses the feeling.

Darkness has come to me,

nighttime has come to me,

darkness has come to me,

but the moon came to me

and made me happy.

My people who look at me,

my ancestors who look back at me,

they are all in the moon

and they swing back and forth

and they are happy.

This same idea was expressed by Peter Tuluk, a man from Chevak also in his thirties. "Since the elders used to tell us

stories about our way of life and what Eskimo songs and dances were, I'd think to myself, 'There's my ancestors singing to me.' It felt like these elders are telling me messages from our ancestors, that's how I really felt: 'Here are my ancestors' and you express them by motion and song."

St. Mary's and Pilot Station are about fourteen miles from each other on the Yukon River. In 1979, on January 16, St. Mary's received an invitation to come to Pilot Station in four days. Even as far away as Bethel I had heard that a potlatch was imminent and I had kept my schedule flexible so that I would be able to get away when the news came. The Twin Otter flew northwest to St. Mary's across the delta. After a half hour of flat whiteness stretching to the horizon in all directions, a dark line of wind-cleared ice, the Yukon, came into view. We landed at the airport on the ridge beyond the village. From there I caught a small mailplane for the fifteen-minute ride to the ridge-top airstrip above Pilot Station. The village flight agent met the plane with his truck. After we climbed out he followed the plane on foot to the end of the runway and braced his arms against a wing, helping the pilot turn the plane around between the narrow confines of the snowberms. He invited me to stay at his home during the potlatch which was to begin that evening.

After supper I took my camera gear to visit and wait at the community hall. The children stationed themselves at the windows, their eyes searching the dark. Finally snowmachine lights were seen coming up river. The lights fluttered back and forth as the drivers maneuvered around rough river ice. Then with a final snarl of the engines, the machines charged up the steep riverbank to the community center. A steady stream of St. Mary's people followed.

The hall suddenly seemed small as the guests swept in, many still dressed in their heavy winter traveling gear. Longtime friends embraced and shook hands. As the room warmed, coats were eventually removed and piled in corners and along the back wall. Gradually about 125 people seated themselves around the perimeter of the room. When all were present a brief welcoming speech was given by the village council president. The host family then presented the child whose name was to be honored.

It was time to bring in the gifts. Armload after armload was carried in by men and placed in a pile in the center of the room. There were many commonly used items such as boxes of detergent, wool socks, rolls of paper towels, cotton work gloves, mops, buckets, and stocking caps. Unwound bolts of colorful cloth were carried in, held high by several men. Finally a few prized gifts were brought in, such as a gun, seal skins, and wolverine pelts. When everyone had had time to admire the gifts they were removed to a back room. With the center of the room cleared, the dancing could begin. This first night the host village would present their new songs as well as many familiar ones.

The drums were brought in first, large hoops of wood with handles. Until a few years earlier drum heads were made from the thin intestinal organ linings of various large marine mammals. However these skins are very responsive to changes in humidity and temperature so that they are difficult to keep in tune. The drum heads at this potlatch were made from clear plastic Visqueen. In the following years I saw various experiments in drum construction but most of these were only brought out for rehearsals. One village tried using bicycle rims for the hoop. I once saw a couple of drums made from galvanized garbage can lids. By now rip-stop nylon, "rainpants," as one man called it, has been almost universally adopted for drum heads. The drummers sit in the traditional line behind the dancers, the drum heads making a row of circles like color samples from some outer-wear catalog—green, cranberry, royal blue, and crimson.

As the four or five drummers seated themselves, a clear piece of spruce was produced. One man pulled out his pocket knife and, with a long controlled stroke, split off a thin stick. Then the knife and wood were passed along to the next drummer. Each man whacked his drum a couple times with his stick to test the sound, stretched the head a little tighter, and positioned a spit can at his feet. Around them the crowd continued to visit. Children rushed around the open dance space as dance fans were removed from plastic bags and placed on the floor for anyone to use. Finally a lone

drumbeat began, accompanied by a thin voice. The other drummers sat unmoving, looking down for a few moments as if to wait for the power of the song to awaken some inner resource. One by one the drummers added their drums and voices until the sound drowned out the noise and everyone was drawn into the beat. Together, they beat the same quarter-note pulse.

A row of seven women placed themselves in a line in front of the drummers. They wore brightly colored *qaspeqs*, cotton tunics decorated with contrasting trim, each made to the individual taste of the dancer. Their headdresses were beaded bands with crowns of long white wolf fur and they held dance fans, woven grass handles decorated with caribou hair, some with waving tufts of swansdown. Bobbing gently at the knees, the women individually found their way into the set of motions that made up the dance. At some impercepti-ble point, all were moving together, the gentle motion of their fans reminiscent of soft grasses in the wind. The women danced with their feet firmly planted on the floor just as their ancestors, confined to the small space of the *qasgiq*, have always done.

One of the men put down his drum and slipped through the line of women. He took the traditional position, kneeling and sitting on his feet in front of them. The man began dancing, his motions the same as those of the women but stronger and more sharply defined. A story was being told, sometimes by the words and always by the motions. The song was repeated several times with the drumbeat increas-ing in volume and speed. The motions, all in practiced uni-son, accelerated until torsos jerked and arms sliced the air wildly. The drumbeats became a physical sensation in our bodies. Then suddenly everything stopped. In a moment the crowd yelled *"pamyua"* meaning "its tail," demanding a more vigorous repetition. Sweating, the dancers resumed their positions and began the song again at a medium tempo. Again each verse topped the previous one in vibrancy until the motions became a blur. Finally the crowd was satisfied and the song was over. Applause and smiles rewarded the ensemble.

The drummers sat silently for a few minutes breathing heavily from exertion and drinking pop or sipping water from a pail placed before them. Then another thin voice and a soft drum beat started up a new song. Some dancers retired into the crowd and others were urged up to do particular songs. Sometimes a single man led the dancers, sometimes groups of men. Some dances were very humorous with the men screwing up their faces to make strange expressions. Eyes rolled and necks turned magically to rubber. Before us were created images of seals diving, of muskrats popping their heads out of water, of birds flying, of dog sled driving, of hunting and shooting. The crowd followed the dances totally, nodding heads, moving hands to the drum, and laughing uproariously when one man jumped into the middle of the dance to imitate another. The room was hot, with momentary waves of cold air slicing through when the door

was opened to relieve the stuffiness. On into the night the dancing continued. A chair was brought out for an old man to sit on as he danced. The children fell asleep one by one in the piles of coats. Some time after midnight the last song ended and everyone filed out into the windy darkness, the guests heading to the homes of friends and relatives.

The next morning the guests were assembled in the hall to receive their gifts. Again, the gifts were piled in the middle of the floor. Then three men started passing them out. Boxes of cigarettes were held in front of each guest so the receiver could select a pack or two. The giving was done with quiet drama, the length of time taken to carry in the gifts adding to the impression. In Yup'ik society it is generally not acceptable to call direct attention to oneself or to other individuals. Emphasis is always placed on the group. So, although eyes quietly measured the gifts and the reactions of the recipients, little outward emotion was shown. The guests continued chatting with friends as items were added to the growing pile in front of each.

The eldest man in the village was handed a stocking cap with the word "turkey" embroidered on it. I don't believe he could read English but, with a comic toothless smile, he quickly pulled it on his head for all to admire. The crowd laughed gently. Women looked over their gifts of clothing and lengths of cloth. To a few elders went highly prized items like seal skins and other furs. Some particularly prized items, like wolverine pelts, were presented to the community in general and were later cut up and distributed to people who needed them. To conclude the giving the hosts passed out plastic garbage bags. The guests loaded their gifts into the bags, collected the children, and began filtering out into the sunshine.

That afternoon the men's potlatch was held in an unheated storage shed. The St. Mary's men silently seated themselves along the wall in rough order according to age and status, the elders on the right progressing to the youngest men on the left. Wearing their heavy outdoor gear, they sat stiffly as the men from Pilot Station brought in gunny sacks of whole frozen salmon and made a pile in the center of the floor.

Andrew Evan and Robert Joe watch dancers, Mountain Village.

Pounding with a hatchet, they separated the fish and placed them one at a time in order on the floor in front of each guest. Then bowls of *akutaq* were brought in and the guests ate without speaking. In the formal silence of the event one of the young men whispered to me that this was the real potlatch, the gifts between men. The *akutaq* was eaten and the fish slipped into plastic bags. At the conclusion the guests stood and thanked their hosts, "*quyana,*" for the gifts and everyone retired for afternoon steam baths.

After a potluck dinner at the village school, the crowd reassembled at the community hall for the second and last night of dancing. Now it was St. Mary's turn, and they danced most of the night. Everyone was more relaxed than the night before and people jumped out of the crowd to participate. Sometimes an invitational song was begun and the whole floor filled with people dancing their own dances. At two in the morning the host dancers began to perform a few final songs and the dancing was over by three. A whirling snowstorm engulfed us all as, badly in need of sleep, we pushed through the deep snow toward our beds.

Aside from the few potlatches that still occur, there has been, since the mid-1970s, a resurgence in native dancing in the delta. In the past, priests and missionaries have tried to eliminate dancing and by the early seventies it was usually limited to the very oldest people in the village and only in the Catholic and Russian Orthodox villages where limits were less successful. The Moravian villages had virtually no dancing at all because it had been so forcefully discouraged by the early missionaries. Neva Rivers from Hooper Bay remembers, "We quit dancing when I was small. All those missionaries came and wiped out all those activities at Hooper Bay. Just like they threatened them with something, made them scared. We started out dancing ever since Mr. Malot, a teacher, started taking pictures in the forties, going around taking pictures and making movies."

In recent years the schools have provided much of the impetus for the resurgence of dance. By the middle of the seventies, with the advent of bilingual education programs in the schools and a rising interest in preserving cultural heri-tage, villagers began encouraging young people to learn dance. Village elders realized that the only people who knew how to dance were getting on in age and they worked to teach the songs to young people so that the tradition would continue. A few of the Moravian villages, after much soul searching and consultation with the church, found ways to begin relearning dance from other villages.

The Yukon villages, beginning with St. Mary's, have been a center for the revival of dancing on the lower Yukon. Andy Paukan is a bilingual teacher from St. Mary's and a leader in this resurgence. He outlined the sequence of events for me that made the large festivals possible. "In 1981 we extended our little [community] hall that we had so it's now forty by sixty feet. We invited Pilot Station and Mountain Village. Everybody had so much fun we decided to invite nine villages the next year. With that accomplished there was talk about hosting a festival to encourage the communities together—try to revive their heritage in dancing." They hosted nine villages in 1982 during a festival that lasted three days. It was such a success that everyone felt it should become a yearly tradition.

In the next few years Mountain Village decided it wanted to host regular dance festivals so the community built an unusually large hall. By 1988 the Lower Yukon Coastal Mayors' Association was in full support of a big festival which was held in the fall of 1989 at the big new hall in Mountain Village. Twelve villages attended. They even were able to arrange to ship ninety Yup'ik artifacts from the Sheldon Jackson Museum in Sitka that had been collected from the area a hundred years ago so that they could be displayed in the village during the potlatch.

Neva Rivers and her sister Helen Smith, both from Hooper Bay, attended the festival and allowed me to tape an interview with the two of them. The dancing and the display of old masks, tools, and fish-skin garments stirred up special memories of the large dances that were held in their village *qasgiq*. Helen described her feelings. "These dance festivals, it makes me happy. Like last night I didn't worry nothing when I saw those dancers. It makes me feel really happy.

Norbert Beans, Mountain Village.

This reminds me of the ones they used to call up. It reminds me of all those things."

Neva and Helen excitedly traded sentences in halting English, remembering when, long before the coming of wood-framed buildings, the largest structure in a village was the *qasgiq*. Built partially underground, the log and sod roof slanted up on all sides with an opening at the top for a smoke hole. The *qasgiq* served as a men's house with a pit in the center where fires were built for bathing. During the summer it was entered by means of a door near ground level. During the winter that door was blocked and the *qasgiq* was entered through a tunnel leading from the outside to the central firepit, an opening that brought fresh air to the fire.

"We danced our own way from our ancestors," began Helen. "It's really a big sod house, everybody would sit down from the oldest down to the youngest men. They would put us children on those shelves on the walls. In winter time they close that main door and then they go underneath down there and come up in the middle of the room [the fire pit]. When us kids come in we hold up our arms and ask them to pull us up. All us children would be really quiet. That *qasgiq* would be just like a holy place. At Hooper Bay, Kashunak [now Chevak] would come over, Kialivik [now Newtok], Scammon Bay—coastal people. They used to walk or go by sled. Not many dogs, maybe one dog. Long time ago they never used to have real dog teams. They used to use one dog and walk at the side of the sled. Most of the people walk. They used to have a big feast sometimes. Lots of *akutaq*, frozen fish, lots of oiled bread. They make all those big pots of tea and everybody eat right there. Five young men would go on top of the *qasgiq*. They make noise, they make lots of noise yelling—just like dog howling. That means tonight they are going to have a really really biggest dance. Bring lots of gifts." Helen continued to describe how once a large figure of a bird, made from sticks and cloth, was made and hung from the ceiling near the dancers. A string attached to the legs would be pulled in time to the drum beat and this large figure moved above their heads.

"And they put it up there at the top of the *qasgiq* and they swing that thing with the drum beat and the legs would move and that thing was real! After, they tie lots of cloth and everything right there. Then every family, the leader, would dance with that headdress downward, over their face and everything. Our daddy was one of the leaders. Then us, my mom, my sister, Neva, and I—Daddy would put one big dry *maklak* seal skin underneath where we could stand up every one of us, and we dance on top of it."

I first believed that the lyrics that were sung to the dances could be directly translated, but I always found it discouraging to have anyone try to interpret and my interpreters often seemed to find it difficult. I gradually came to realize that much of the story is told through motions alone and that many of the words are extended to mark the rhythm or have evolved from ancient sources to the point that meanings are vague. I also assumed at first that the songs and dances were all very old, passed down through many generations. But then at a dance in Bethel in 1975, I saw Nick Ashepak do a hilarious dance wearing a wig, earrings made from dog chain clips, and a grass skirt that someone brought back from Hawaii. It was a simple story that he made up with his friend Peter Jacobs. The dance described a lady getting all dressed up to go out on the town. She went outside and pulled three times on the starter rope of her snowmachine and then drove around town "real fast."

In the past ten years in Chevak, dance has become a very important part of the school program. Villagers recognize its continuing social contribution. "When we're dancing we're entertaining," Peter Tuluk explained to me at the 1989 dance festival in Mountain Village. "We're going to make them feel good, get rid of their tensions, their frustrations and the bad things that happened, sort of like healing the other person." One common way that Yup'iks accomplish this is with teasing and laughter. The institution of teasing, especially between certain cousins, plays a big part. Peter continued, "Those teasing cousins are out there too and they are going to want to make you dance until you probably drop. They yell '*pamyua*' or '*cali*' [demanding a repetition] which means you made a mistake. Even if you know the whole song you are bound to make a mistake. If a teasing cousin doesn't dance, then they just keep quiet because they know we'll get them in some other way."

Once on a visit to Nightmute a friend, Liz Joe, told me how she opened the back door of her house one day to dispose of a pan of dirty dish water. She threw the water out and the wind caught it and blew it all back on her. Sheepishly she looked around and, to her relief, she saw no one. That night there was dancing at the school and a dance had been composed about the whole event. Someone had been watching.

Since basketball is now so popular in all the villages, there are numerous basketball songs. And there are songs about broken outboards, chewing gum, teachers, and movies. David Friday described a favorite humorous song. "There was this time when a family raised a crane at Chevak. It didn't fly south in the fall. When the planes come in, at that time a lot of people used to go meet the plane just to see who was on it, almost the whole village. Along with the people there used to be that crane that would walk up with them. It used to strike me—all these people walking up to the airport and there was a crane walking along with them going to check the plane. So my dad made a song. They'd unload the plane and then the crane would fly away. They have a motion for crane that goes to the airport to check the plane and then the crane would fly back to the village. I couldn't forget that song!"

He also mentioned an important difference between old and new songs. "Most of the songs are made to entertain, like my dad says that nowadays the Eskimo dance is to make people happy and get their minds off what's troubling them. The purposes before were like, shamans composing their songs for getting food."

However, the contemporary songs still serve important traditional purposes. Songs were sometimes used for public correction of misdeeds, especially at the celebration of *kevgiq* (Morrow 1984:133). As Andy Paukan explained, "All the songs that are made have the intention to have the guests listen to them, just like telling a story. Ideals are conveyed, experi-

ences, frustrations within the community are conveyed."
To illustrate his point, Andy talked about a song by Mary
Mike, one of the elderly ladies in St. Mary's. "The people are
going to bingo leaving their families behind because of the
give-aways and thousand-dollar jackpots. She made that song
up three years ago. When the people heard it they kind of
had their faces down, their eyes down saying, 'That's really
true. This lady's telling us that we're spending too much time
in the bingo halls.' They can go to a meeting and express
their opinions to the mayor or the village council president
and it would not have as much impact as a song. That is
to us very important."

Peter Tuluk recited for me a song on the subject of making
life choices. It struck me as an especially poignant song in
these times of change on the delta.

My drum is taking me here,

My drum is flying me there,

But should I follow it or should I not?

"It's a song about the drum leading your life, like should
I follow this way of life, or follow that way of life? One way
the drum is leading me in the way that is good, and the
other way leads to confusion. At the end the choice is there.
You can go this way or that and that's the end of the song."

The songs give excellent information about living off
the land, but more than that, they celebrate the spirit of subsistence, the Yup'iks' reciprocal relationship with their environment and the animals with whom they share the land.
Chuna McIntyre told me a hunting song by William Tyson
from the St. Mary's area on the Yukon. "It's a song composed
at the turn of the century when guns were introduced."

It slowly circles me,

the endeared emperor goose who circles me.

Here I sit on this small piece of detached earth,

a piece of tundra floating on the river.

I wave to that bird and it comes this way.

So what do I do?

Obviously, I hunt it with my gun.

It slowly circles me,

the endeared Canadian goose who circles me.

Here I sit on this small piece of detached earth.

I don't want that silly bird but it comes this way.

So what do I do?

Obviously, I hunt it.

A song recited for me by David Bill, a dancer and drummer
from Toksook Bay, explains needlefishing. Needlefish are a
small, oily species found in abundance in some places along
the coast. As he says, "It tells a story to the younger people
who don't know about it.

"You go out in the morning, hitch up your dogs to go
needlefishing in any kind of weather, good weather, bad
weather. The needlefish you have to look for them in certain
tides that bring them in and out. Putting a hole in the ice,
fixing up your dipnet, dipping it in and pulling them out and
you finally fill up your sled. If the weather is bad you stay
there. If the weather is good you go home, day or night.
Some of the needlefish you get you're supposed to feed to
your family and most of it to your dogs."

One of David Friday's favorites is "about a person who
goes out and pulls up his *qaspeq* to his waist. He has a dipnet
and goes down to the river and catches lots of salmon. Then
he puts them up on the bank and cuts them up, then hangs
them up, and looks at them and inspects them. That's a song
I relate to most. I danced that song when my dad first made
that song. I grew up subsisting and that song brings the
orientation to me in the modern world. That's probably why
I enjoy that dance the most."

Just as this book was being completed I talked with Theresa John from Toksook Bay, daughter of Paul John. Now

in her thirties, Theresa does subsistence and commercial fishing during the summer and is studying for an advanced degree in education. She teaches Yup'ik dance at the University of Alaska at Fairbanks. She recited a song for me composed by her grandfather, Teddy Moses. Theresa says, "I really listen to [his songs] at times because he's so expressive emotionally." This song is particularly important to her and it speaks to me as well. It poses questions that anyone working in the arctic might ask.

Here I am walking in the cold weather,

going to a movie and the wind is blowing.

What am I doing out here?

Here I am,

I find myself walking in the middle of town,

and it's a white-out and it's blowing,

and I can't find the house.

Why am I here?

"The song eventually ends by saying—this is why I'm doing this, because I'm a human being and because it was laid there in front of me, and I am to go through it. So here I am presenting these situations to you."

Theresa Charles, *Cama-i* Dance Festival, Bethel.

Acknowledgments

IN 1985 I MENTIONED TO GARY HOLTHAUS, THEN director of the Alaska Humanities Forum, that I was thinking about producing a book. He pounced on my suggestion and introduced me to Naomi Pascal of the University of Washington Press. Naomi's sustained confidence and her approach to seeing the project through remind me of the Yup'ik way of working. For the best results, everything happens in its time without mind-muddying hurry and with the greatest of trust in the process. I thank her for her confidence and patience. Our editor, Lane Morgan, did wonders. When Yup'ik women make *akutaq*, they carefully texture its surface with a spoon to make it perfectly inviting. Lane did likewise with the text. I would also like to thank Audrey Meyer and Julidta Tarver of the University of Washington Press.

My wife Robin, who assisted in writing the text, must be recognized as a partner in the whole book. We shared many of the experiences and then relived them together in the writing. I roughed it out and she wove it all together adding much as she went. We think of this as our book.

Always beside us in Bethel and now Fairbanks have been our close friends Phyllis Morrow and Chase Hensel. They are anthropologists and linguists, who read and commented on the manuscript and patiently answered numerous hurried telephone queries. More importantly, we lived and grew in tandem during our Bethel years, sharing ideas and know-how on every subject from Yup'ik table manners to snowmachine repair to the ethics of living and working where we were. It is perhaps in this last matter that Phyllis and Chase have provided the best inspiration.

Ann Fienup-Riordan has produced extensive anthropological descriptions on the Yup'iks which were an invaluable resource, and she provided much appreciated advice. She and I worked together at times in the villages. Her unremitting energy and cheerfulness were as much appreciated as her belief in my work. Richard Nelson's interest in my photography and his encouragement to work with my field notes helped determine the book's form in its early stages. Another writer, Caroline Kremmer, gave the book a reading at the end.

I owe a special thanks to Elsie Mather, whose documentation of her people's mythology has been a lifetime commitment. Her careful reading of the manuscript was a great help. Theresa John, a teacher of Yup'ik dance, did a similar reading. Thanks also are due to another dancer, Chuna McIntyre, for his insightful comments. These two performers, knowing the importance of a good ending, helped give the final chapter life.

To lifetime Bethel resident Paul Gregory I owe thanks of a different sort. The story begins with a man riding in his dog sled, an inspiration to stay and make my home on the delta. I now believe that was Paul. The project closed with Paul's public support, his expressed hope that the book "could help others to understand what we do in our villages to live our way of life, subsisting off of our lands." Paul is a sophisticated observer of non-Yup'iks. I once introduced a visiting classical guitarist to Paul while he was working with his dog team. Questioned about the names of his dogs, Paul grinned, "This is a bilingual team." Along with the Yup'ik names were his best female, Jane Fonda, and his toughest male, Clint Eastwood.

Mary Pete brought her exceptional skills as a subsistence user, scientist, and anthropologist to her reading and critique. Her knowledge of the legal and political history of the area was invaluable. I am honored that she was willing to write the Foreword, given her extraordinarily busy schedule.

There were others from outside the delta, with various points of view, who gave their time to read the manuscript. I'm grateful for the editorial skills and encouragement of

Robin's family, Herb, Betty, and Holly M. Bailey. They are a rare blessing, in-laws who know exactly when and how to help. Also, special thanks go to my mother and my brother Tom and his wife Doris for their support. Nancy Rabener gave the manuscript several rounds of determined editing at different stages. Nancy, herself a photographer, gave me invaluable help with photoediting at a time, late in the project, when I felt I could no longer see my own work. Steve Jacobson, author of the *Yup'ik Eskimo Dictionary*, shared his knowledge and time as we grappled with the lunar complexities of the chapter headings. Ann-Lillian Schell brought her familiarity with the delta to her cartography. Unseen is the wizardry of Geoffrey Orth, who always stabilized our computer.

Numerous other people contributed to the book by consenting to be interviewed or by providing information. They include: Pete Abruska, Alice Abraham, John Active, Paul Agimuk, Nick Alexie, Paul Alexie, Edward Aloysius, Carlie Akerelrea, Gemma Akerelrea, John Amadeus, Regina Andrews, Matthew Beans, David Bill, Teddy Brink, Marie Brite, Agnes Kelly Bostrum, Wilber Bunyon, Bucky Burrows, Nick Charles, Walkie Charles, Francis and Theresa Charlie, Joe Chief, Andrew Chikoyak, Joe Coffee, Chris and Margaret Cooke, George Dan, Joe and Lucy Demantle, Willy Duny, Peter Dull, William Dull, Kriska Evans, Jacky Feigon, David Friday, Phillip Foxie, Clyde Francis, Robert Gibson, Betty Guy, Allan Hanson, Charles Hanson, John Hanson, John and Olive Hawk, Edward Hooper, Marius Hofseth, Anesia Hoover and family, Homer Hunter, Dan Joe, Liz Joe, Paul John, Simeon John, Clem Joseph, Louise Kanrilak, Bruno and Theresa Kasayulie, Sebastian Kasayulie, Damian Keotok, Alma Keyes, Carl Kawagley, Billy Lincoln Sr., Joe Lincoln, Adolph and Maggie Lind, Austin and Rose Mathias, Ignatius Mathias, George Nevak, Alex Nick, Peter Nick, Joe Paniak, Andy Paukan, Frank Pete, Isadore and Laura Pete, Willy Pitka, Joe Phillip, Patrick Phillip, Noel Polty, Joe Post, Leonard and Mary Raymond, Billy and Alice Rivers, Neva Rivers, Sinka Sakar, John Samuelson, Dennis and Winnie Sheldon, Pat and Nikki Shelp, Clyde Smith, Helen Smith, Paul Tony, Peter Tuluk, Tony Ulak, Al and Maggie Wasuli, Gordon Westlock, Harry Wilson, and Frances Usugan.

My greatest debt and gratitude obviously go to the people of the delta. I could never thank everyone who fed me tea, told me stories, taught me how to fix a bad gasket, gave me a warm bed, or saved my skin on the sea ice. I have always tried to busy myself in small ways to reciprocate for my hosts' generosity. This book is one of those gestures.

James H. Barker

Bibliography

THE FOLLOWING IS A LIST OF SOURCES THAT WERE especially helpful in preparing the introductory section of this book. Also included are general readings on the subject that may be of interest.

Berger, Thomas R.
1985   *Village Journey: The Report of the Alaska Native Review Commission.* New York: Hill and Wang.

Brooks, Alfred H.
1953   *Blazing Alaska Trails.* Fairbanks: University of Alaska Press.

Collier, John, Jr.
1973   *Alaskan Eskimo Education.* New York: Holt, Rinehart and Winston.

Curtis, Edward
1930   *The North American Indian. Vol. 20.* Norwood, Mass.: Plimpton Press. (Reprinted 1976, New York/San Francisco/London: Johnson Reprint Corp.)

Drebert, Ferdinand
1959   *Alaska Missionary.* Bethlehem, Penn. (Reprinted 1971 by Lehigh Litho Inc. and distributed by the Moravian Book Shop.)

Dumas, David, ed.
1984   *Handbook of North American Indians. Vol. 5, Arctic.* Washington, D.C.: Smithsonian Institution.
        This volume describes different Eskimo groups from the Western Arctic across Canada to Greenland, providing a broad framework for understanding individual subgroups. Included are two articles by James VanStone on mainland Yup'iks and another by Margaret Lantis on Nunivak Islanders.

Fienup-Riordan, Ann
1990   *Eskimo Essays.* New Brunswick and London: Rutgers University Press.
        Essays ranging in subject from subsistence ideology and cosmology to western religious influence to warfare, law, and ecology. Each essay helps to put into perspective traditional Yup'ik world views and contemporary responses to different issues. Myths about Eskimo people are addressed.

1984   "Regional Groups on the Yukon-Kuskokwim Delta." *Études/Inuit/Studies* (Quebec) 8:63–93.

1983   *The Nelson Island Eskimo: Social Structure and Ritual Distribution.* Anchorage: Alaska Pacific University Press.
        The first chapter gives a synopsis of the historical period including information on early contact, education, religion, and the economics of subsistence. Chapter 2 covers a year's subsistence cycle. The rest of the book covers social, ritual, and ideological factors relating to subsistence.

1982   *When Our Bad Season Comes: A Cultural Account of Subsistence Harvesting and Harvest Disruption on the Yukon Delta.* Anchorage: Alaska Anthropological Association, Monograph Series #1.
        An ethnographic account of subsistence in the Yukon Delta, with detailed descriptions of how species are harvested. Examines the correlation between social history and land use patterns and projects the impact of possible harvest disruption caused by either natural phenomena or development.

Fitzhugh, William W., and Aron Crowell
1988   *Crossroads of Continents: Cultures of Siberia and Alaska.* Washington, D.C.: Smithsonian Institution Press.
        A catalog written to accompany a historic Smithsonian exhibit of artifacts collected on both sides of the Bering Strait. Examines precontact times and the relationships of the various North Pacific culture groups. The functions and social meaning of the many artifacts are discussed in articles by contem-

porary ethnographers. Of particular interest to those wanting more information on current issues is an essay on Alaska Natives today by Rosita Whorl.

Fitzhugh, William W., and Susan A. Kaplan
1982   *Inua: Spirit World of the Bering Sea Eskimo.* Washington, D.C.: Smithsonian Institution Press.
A catalog for the Smithsonian's Bering Sea Eskimo artifacts collected by Edward Nelson in his travels during 1877–81. Taken from his field notes but also incorporating works by contemporary anthropologists, the book covers daily life, legends, religion, and art as encountered at that time. It provides background on the ideology of subsistence as well as beautiful photographs of numerous artifacts.

Henkelman, James W., and Kurt Vitt
1985   *Harmonious to Dwell: The History of the Alaska Moravian Church 1885–1985.* Bethel, Alaska: Moravian Seminary and Archives.

Henning, Robert A., ed.
1979   *Yukon Kuskokwim Delta, Alaska Geographic,* vol. 6, no. 1.
This volume in a series on different culture groups in the state is an excellent photographic introduction to the area. It includes a summary of the region's history, descriptions of contemporary village life, and information on subsistence and social change.

Jacobson, Steven A.
1984   *Yup'ik Eskimo Dictionary.* Fairbanks: Alaska Native Language Center, University of Alaska.

Kalikaq Yugnek, Inc.
1977   *Kalikaq Yugnek,* Bethel, Alaska: Bethel Regional High School, Lower Kuskokwim School District.

Lenz, Mary, and James H. Barker
1985   *Bethel: The First 100 Years,* Bethel, Alaska: City of Bethel.
A history of the town of Bethel as a center of contact and social change in the region. Contains numerous historical photographs. An outline of the community's political, religious, and social history frames numerous stories and quotes taken from journals, letters, and taped interviews.

Morgan, Lael, ed.
1979   *Alaska's Native People, Alaska Geographic,* vol. 6, no. 3.

Morrow, Phyllis
1984   "It Is Time for Drumming: A Summary of Recent Research on Yup'ik Ceremonialism." *Études/Inuit/Studies* (Quebec) 8:113–40.
A summary of a book published in Yup'ik by Elsie Mather, *Cauyarnariuq,* which compiles Mather's newly collected materials on the annual cycle of Yup'ik ceremonies. Morrow's discussion expands on the somewhat incomplete and sometimes confused reports of early ethnographers. Her careful analysis of ritual meanings is helpful to readers interested in understanding Yup'ik ways of viewing the world.

Nelson, Edward W.
1899   *The Eskimo about Bering Strait.* Bureau of American Ethnology, Annual Report, vol. 18, pt. 1. Washington, D.C.: Smithsonian Institution.
Chronicles Nelson's four years of travel and observation from 1877 to 1881, much of it in the Yukon-Kuskokwim region. Includes a wealth of detailed description on a wide variety of ethnographic subjects, many drawings and photographs, and a collection of folklore.

Nickerson, Sheila, ed.
1989   "Alaskans' per Capita Harvests of Wild Food." *Alaska Fish & Game* 21 (no. 6): 14–15.

Nunam Kitlusisti
1984   *Just a Small Fishery: The Cape Romanzof District Commercial Herring Fishery.* Robin Bailey Barker and James H. Barker, eds. Bethel, Alaska: Nunam Kitlusisti, a subsidiary of the Association of Village Council Presidents.
1982   *"The Issue Is Survival": A Summary of Yukon-Kuskokwim Delta Villagers' Testimony and Concerns Addressing Federal and State Off Shore Oil Lease Sale Plans for the Norton Sound Basin in the Bering Sea, Alaska, Seeking a Five Year Delay.* James

H. Barker, ed. Bethel, Alaska: Nunam Kitlusisti.

1981 *You Don't Forget Hunger: In Support of Subsistence Harvest of Herring on Nelson Island, Western Alaska.* Mary Lenz and James H. Barker, eds. Bethel, Alaska: Nunam Kitlusisti.

1977 *". . . a Special Relationship with the Land."* James H. Barker, ed. Bethel, Alaska: Nunam Kitlusisti.

1976 *"I Feel Like I'm Just Wasting My Breath": Testimonies Spoken by Western Alaskans to the Bureau of Land Management.* James H. Barker, ed. Bethel, Alaska: Nunam Kitlusisti.

Oswalt, Wendell H.

1963 *Mission of Change in Alaska.* San Marino, Calif.: Huntington Library.

1980 *Kolmakovskiy Redoubt.* Monumenta Archaeologica, vol. 8. Los Angeles: Institute of Archaeology, University of California.

1990 *Bashful No Longer: An Alaskan Eskimo Ethnohistory, 1778–1988.* Norman and London: University of Oklahoma Press.
Traces Yup'ik contact with Westerners in the Kuskokwim villages from the early Russian period through Americanization up to 1988. It begins with a description of precontact culture and goes on to give detailed information on missionary influence, education, economics, and politics over the years.

Pete, Mary C.

1989 "The Universe in a Mask." *Alaska Fish & Game* 21 (no. 6): 38.

Ray, Dorothy Jean

1975 *The Eskimo of Bering Strait, 1650–1898.* Seattle: University of Washington Press.

Schwalbe, Anna B.

1951 *Dayspring on the Kuskokwim.* Bethlehem, Penn.: Moravian

Church in America. (Reprinted 1985. Gertrude Trodahl and Harry Trodahl, eds.)

Shinkwin, Anne, and Mary C. Pete

1983 *Homes in Disruption: Spouse Abuse in Yup'ik Eskimo Society.* Fairbanks: University of Alaska.

1984 "Yup'ik Eskimo Societies: A Case Study." *Études/Inuit/Studies* (Quebec) 8:95–112.

Treca, Joseph M., S.J.

1890 Letter to a friend, 3-4-1890. Oregon Province Archives, Spokane, Washington.

Wolfe, Robert J.

1982 "Alaska's Great Sickness, 1900: An Epidemic of Measles and Influenza in a Virgin Soil Population." *Proceedings of the American Philosophical Society* 126 (2): 91–121.

Wolfe, Robert J., and Robert J. Walker

1987 "Subsistence Economies in Alaska: Productivity, Geography, and Development Impacts." *Arctic Anthropology* 24 (no. 2): 56–81.
A summary of subsistence surveys throughout Alaska, this article looks at the contribution of subsistence to the economies of rural communities in the 1980s. Detailed analysis of size, composition, and location of harvests is made and the relationship of subsistence to development is discussed.

Yukon-Kuskokwim Health Corporation

1974 *"I Can't Tell You Before You Ask Me."* Cheryl Roussain, ed. Bethel, Alaska: Yukon-Kuskokwim Health Corporation.

Zagoskin, Lavrentii P.

1967 *Lieutenant Zagoskin's Travels in Russian America 1842–1844.* Henry N. Michael, ed. Toronto: University of Toronto Press, published for the Arctic Institute of North America.

Mary and Jack Stewart flying home to Goodnews Bay.